Modern Nordic

Contemporary recipes
from a Scandinavian kitchen

SIMON BAJADA

Hardie Grant
BOOKS

METEOROLOGEN
SKI LODGE · RIKSGRÄNSEN · LAPPLAND

PREFACE

Born in Australia and now living in Sweden, Simon Bajada is as much a creator of modern Nordic cuisine as any Dane, Swede, Finn or Greenlander. His deep curiosity about cooking and eating habits in our region, and the years he has spent travelling around the Arctic region, have turned him from an observer into a contributor. His contribution is clearly evident in the recipes on these pages, which reflect both Simon's contemporary understanding of the Nordic spirit and his relentless love for our landscape.

—

Simon's ability to detect uniqueness in techniques and flavours, as well as aesthetics, comes at least partly from the fact that he wasn't born and raised in the Nordic region. He arrived with a different cultural education and has used that to his advantage. What we take for granted in everyday life, he finds special. He captures and develops the small details to which we are inured, then feeds them back to us so that we can cherish and harbour them. This is perhaps the essence of how a food culture grows.

In ancient times, the recipes and food-related rituals in the Nordic region were purely acts of survival. Nutrients over delicacy, preservation over freshness, nurturing over refinement. As our culture grew more civilised and cosmopolitan, many of these aspects disappeared. But some primary techniques and flavours have remained, in more sophisticated forms. Our love of preservation and fermentation is flourishing, as is our celebration of winter cooking over fire.

The Nordic devotion to spices such as cardamom, cinnamon and star anise stems from the return, hundreds of years ago, of the first ships to travel from Europe to India and East Asia. Without knowing how these scents and flavours were used in their native regions, we started to use them for baking, in drinks or, in the case of sandalwood, to flavour herring (surely an alien concept in Asia, both then and now). Just as we were once inspired by our travels abroad, now is the moment for Nordic food culture to inspire the rest of the planet.

The Nordic approach to home cooking never depended on precise measures or exact temperatures. Rather, it has always relied on feeling your way forward, and using whatever you have on hand, to create what you think will taste good. Simon's recipes are a wonderful foundation for your journey into Nordic food. I encourage you to use them to experiment with flavours and explore your own ideas – to feel your way forward into modern Nordic cookery.

Mattias Kroon

CONTENTS

INTRODUCTION 06

Basics *10*

Larder *38*

Classics *66*

From the Sea *108*

From the Land *148*

From the Forest *190*

Baking *218*

Sweets *258*

THE REPLACEMENTS 296

INDEX 298

INTRODUCTION

Yes, this is a book full of recipes to cook from, but it is much more than only that. Through the ingredients and methods used, as well as the stories and anecdotes woven throughout, I want to give you an understanding of the food and cooking techniques enjoyed across the region so that you can bring a little Nordic style into your own kitchen and home.

—

In the mid 2000s, a new cuisine emerged seemingly out of nowhere. The Nordic countries, long respected for their contributions to social equality and beautiful design, had seldom been recognised for their food. That changed when a group of chefs from various Nordic countries declared a manifesto that revolutionised the culinary landscape. The core message was simple: *eat local.* Why import a mango to Copenhagen when you have an abundance of delicious berries right on your doorstep?

The cuisine sent ripples through the culinary world, and many of the restaurants embracing the manifesto continue to earn awards and feature on top restaurant lists today. Ironically, chefs all over, even in tropical regions, began pickling and preserving, not out of necessity – to extend the shelf life of fruits or smoked fish for long winters – but because cooking this way had been popularised.

While food trends come and go, and the spotlight on Nordic chefs may have dimmed in recent years, there's no doubt that modern Nordic cuisine is here to stay. Its influence has transformed the culinary scene throughout the world while inspiring a new generation of home cooks and diners across the region to appreciate high-quality cooking. Palates have become more educated, and the standards for food have been elevated – all thanks to this groundbreaking cuisine.

When I'm asked, 'What is modern Nordic cuisine?' I don't have an easy answer, but I have some thoughts on what it is *not.* It is not a fusion of cuisines, nor is it a simple reinterpretation of Nordic classics. It is not an entirely new set of flavours either. Rather, it centres on an idea. It is a celebration of traditional Nordic methods of sourcing local ingredients – from foraging to fishing and hunting – and preparing them in new, but tried and tested, ways. I would describe the flavours as earthy, clean and subtle, often with soft contrasts of sweet and sour.

This book is not a rhapsody on the wonders of Nordic cooking and it doesn't intend to be a potted history of the region. My hope is simply that it plants a seed and inspires you to think beyond the cuisines with which you are already familiar. You may cook a recipe and think: 'That would be better with ...' Well, go ahead and change it! Play around with the flavours. The only rule I tried to abide by when putting together these recipes was to use ingredients common to Northern Europe. Of course, Nordic folk don't only cook with ingredients and products from their own region, but I think local ingredients bring an authenticity to these dishes, giving us a clearer understanding of the distinctive flavours from the area. Of course you can use olive oil if you have run out of rapeseed oil; just consider that the taste will be different and understand why. The Basics and Larder chapters (see pages 10–37 and 38–65) will familiarise you with how ingredients are used and what their unique properties can bring to a dish, and as you proceed through the chapters I hope you will gain a deeper understanding of how to prepare and serve your own modern Nordic dishes.

A phrase has stuck with me ever since a Nordic chef placed a plate in front of me and said, 'Now, we are taking you to the forest floor.' And the dish did just that: the mushrooms and other wonderfully earthy ingredients took me straight there. Modern Nordic cuisine mirrors its landscape – raw, subtle, grounded, just like the vast treeless plains of Iceland or the rocky outcrops of the many archipelagos scattered around the coasts. The beauty of the region doesn't tend to stop you in your tracks, but it will always make you look twice. It will creep up on you until you truly appreciate its harmony and subtle complexity, just like its cuisine.

CHAPTER ONE

Basics

Classic Nordic gastronomy has a long tradition of looking outwards, adopting those well-practised skills from Western Europe. I will revisit these through the recipes in the following chapters, updating them to reflect our ever-changing tastes. I will also explore some of the wonderful newer techniques developed in recent years, many of which are helping make Nordic cooking more accessible at home.

New Nordic cooking aims to achieve a perfect balance of sweet, sour, salty, bitter and umami. Sometimes this is simply through the clever use of a quickly pickled garnish to offset a sweeter dish; or it could be via a more complex layering of flavours. To make things even more interesting though, the lines between sweet and savoury are often blurred, with flourishes of each dotted throughout.

Ingredients are typically Northern European, by which I mean that they grow well in a cold climate. In the past there has been a surge in interest in what the chilly, often sparse Nordic habitat can bring to the dining table, and with coastlines and forests ripe for harvesting, foraging is a popular endeavour. I encourage you to look at what is growing around you and all that is local to your environment.

In this section, I will introduce you to some of the principal ideas behind new Nordic cuisine: the equipment you will need and ingredients you'll come across, and explore how traditional techniques such as pickling, smoking and curing have found a place in contemporary kitchens.

Equipment

As in all cooking, the use of different ingredients gives rise to different preparation methods, which in turn often require a different set of tools.

As well as the methods from the past fifty years or so,those classical French and other Western-European styles with which we are all so familiar – chefs of the new Nordic cuisine have started to look back even further for inspiration. Some cook using heat from hot rocks set into pits dug into the ground, the food wrapped in birch tree bark; others cook in cast-iron pots set over open fires. And there is a restaurant I know where they only use flame and smoke. These ancient techniques, mixed in with the new, are helping to define what new Nordic cuisine is and can be.

The new Nordic home kitchen doesn't require masses of fancy kit, but there are a few tools that will help produce the best results, and bring authenticity to your cooking.

Cast-iron pans & casseroles

At one time, Sweden produced the best quality coal and as a result of this industry they also perfected the art of cast-iron. Old cookbooks passed down through the generations all call for the use of this sturdy cookware, and for many good reasons. Using a flimsy non-stick pan means the base gets very hot, very quickly which, when making a batch of now-famous Nordic meatballs, for example, can lead to burning and patchy cooking. Cast-iron gives a well-rounded even temperature, ensuring the meat cooks all the way through with less direct heat. As an added benefit, the cookware acts as a natural iron enrichment, a mineral that many of us lack in our modern-day diets.

Cast-iron is a reliable, long-lasting material that, with a little care, can be used over and over again. Eventually, though, after repeated use, your pan will dry out, and when this happens, or if you happen to score a winning second-hand one, it's easy to re-season. Pour a thin layer of rapeseed oil into the dry pan then heat to a high temperature, either on the stove or in the oven, depending on whether the handle is heatproof. After about 10–15 minutes, when the oil has stopped smoking, the pan will be black and properly seasoned again, ready for use.

Cast-iron cooking utensils are available in many different shapes for use over fire or on the stove top.

GEFLE

Mandoline

We have all seen flourishing garnishes, waving delicately from atop artful smears on our plates. Sometimes these garnishes are so thin one can't even tell what they are. The trick to achieving these very thin shards of 'whatever' is to use a mandoline. It's a great tool, allowing you to play around with raw and pickled ingredients to all manner of decorative effects. These types of garnishes almost always adorn new Nordic dishes and they offer up more than just their looks; they also add important texture and acidity, as they are usually pickled. Try shaping these with a knife and chopping board and you'll find it a very hard task. Throughout the book you will see plenty of examples of garnishes sliced using a mandoline.

Cheese slicer

In 1925, Norwegian inventor Thor Bjørklund introduced us to the Nordic cheese slicer. His design drew influence from the carpenter's plane, enabling you to shave off very thin slices. It is essential in the everyday eating of open sandwiches (see pages 71–5). Its uses extend beyond cheese though, making it a great addition to any kitchen. It can also be used like a mandoline to slice vegetables very thinly – just be very careful! If you do acquire one, sooner or later you will know what I mean when I say your cheese wedge looks like a ski jump.

Danish rye bread guillotine

Danish bread can be dense, so dense that a normal bread knife can make hard work of cutting slices. This specialist slicer makes the task easier. A Danish company called Raadvad have been making them since the nineteenth century and they are available online.

Pickling jars & stoneware pots

These were mandatory when preserving food was essential to keep going through the seasons, and they are still used today. Jars need to have a sealed lid for pickles and brines; the pots are for preserving berry jams and compotes.

Notched rolling pin

These famous bread pins, called *kruskavel*, are from Sweden and they put the dimples in flatbreads that help them cook more evenly. They come in two different depths of textures, depending on what type of bread you are making. Crispbreads use a more pointed dimple version, so the hot air can reach a greater surface area, and the other less-defined type is used for softer flatbreads. If you cannot find a *kruskavel* you can always use the back of a fork to make your dimples.

Egg slicer

While the rest of the world enjoys a yolk oozing out on to some sourdough, Nordic countries love a hard-boiled egg. This slicer uses a wire frame to cut perfectly even slices and it is essential to the ritual of open sandwiches (see pages 71–5). The large Swedish furniture retailer sells them cheaply.

Swedish butter knife, *smörknivar*

These special butter knives are made from open-grained, flexible wood with a slight scent of a fresh spring forest. The finish of the wood is very smooth and you can get them in many different shapes, but the most important design feature is that the blade is wider than the handle.

The thickness of the knife is also important. This allows you to achieve the right flex when scooping up butter with a precise sweeping motion, and to apply sufficient resistance when spreading the butter on bread.

It is said that some families in Sweden even have individual butter knives! And I've also read that if you tarnish a knife with anything other than butter it must be thrown away!

Decilitre (DL) to cups converter

Traditionally, Nordic countries use a metric system that differs from grams, millilitres or cups. They use a special measuring device for both wet and dry ingredients. I haven't used them in this book, but for any future Nordic recipes you come across, 1 decilitre (DL) is equal to 100 ml (3½ fl oz).

Whole & raw foods

Being spoiled for choice can limit our creativity. I think the harsh Nordic climate, with its restricted range of produce has actively encouraged chefs to think imaginatively and develop new techniques for preparing traditional and familiar ingredients. I will probably say this many times in this book in one way or another, but 'old ingredients–new ideas' is a good summation of the mentality of new Nordic cooking.

Familiar techniques are not being disregarded, but perhaps they are being questioned. Nordic chefs feel free to try new things without being held down by a strict heritage of how things are 'meant to be done', as one might find in other, classical European cuisines.

The recent and growing popularity of raw food, primarily due to perceived nutritional benefits, is very fitting for Nordic cuisine as it opens the doors to what can be done with backyard produce. And working with the seasons is tied directly to this: the freshest ingredients will give you the best flavours.

Combine this 'raw' approach with the Nordic loves of pickling and cooking with fire and coal, and all of a sudden a parsnip can be presented in ten delicious ways.

Chefs are also thinking at either end of the scale – in one dish you might find just a few raw fronds of broccoli acting as a garnish, while in another a whole slow-roasted celeriac could be your centrepiece. These sorts of ideas are springing up in new Nordic kitchens at a rapid rate. Some may not stand the test of time, but it is the experimentation that is so exciting; the better ones will stick, and the others won't.

You'll find lots of unusual ideas in the upcoming chapters, but I'm not going to provide a comprehensive list of them here. Through reading this book and cooking from it, I hope you will learn something of the new Nordic way of thinking, so that you, at home, can develop your own ideas for serving everyday ingredients in different and surprising ways. Come at an ingredient from a different perspective and try something you've never thought of before. Perhaps toast a few grains of buckwheat rather than pine nuts to add crunch to a salad, or serve slices of raw mushrooms to add an earthy texture to a dish. Some of your adventures in the kitchen might not work, but some might open up an entirely new way of cooking for you.

Key ingredients

Dairy products are an everyday part of the Nordic diet – there are more than double the varieties of milk products across the region than can be found in most countries. Of particular interest is their range of **sour** and **fermented milks**. Due to their limited availability outside Nordic countries, some of the recipes ahead use a mixture of yoghurt and milk to reach a similar density and flavour. **Yoghurts, creams, butters** and **cheeses** are all intrinsic to the Nordic diet and you will see them appearing time and again in the recipes in this book.

Flour is not limited to one variety; the list is long. **Buckwheat**, **rye** and **Graham flour** (a form of wholemeal [whole-wheat] flour) and many other wheat flours available in a huge array of textures and densities result in a diverse selection of breads.

With such a large coastline and with many inland waterways, **fish** and **seafood** feature highly in Nordic cuisine. The varieties of fish that are found in the region (mainly oily and/or firm-fleshed) lend themselves well to traditional preservation techniques, such as brining, smoking, pickling and curing (see pages 22–37). **Salmon** and **herring** are the most common, but **trout** and **small prawns** (or shrimp) are also popular.

Traditional Nordic cooking, like many other Western food cultures, has always relied heavily on the meat component in a dish. This is changing and new Nordic cooking is shifting its focus. **Beef** and **lamb**, although quite expensive, are still used though, and **pork**, which is less expensive due to its intense production, is heavily consumed. **Poultry**, in comparison to other Western cultures, is rather insignificant. With endless forests, game meats such as **venison** and **elk** are popular at home as well as appearing on many restaurant menus.

Since the range of **vegetables** able to grow this far north is limited, new Nordic chefs – who are keen locavores – have become very creative in their preparation techniques. Cold-climate vegetables that you'll find used across the region include **cabbage, cauliflower, onions, beetroot** (or beets) and **radish**. **Swede** (or rutabaga) and other native root vegetables are very popular.

The **potato** is ever-present in Nordic cuisine. This humble hero, eaten, with its thin skin, is a treat in itself, especially when newly harvested around midsummer.

The **cucumber** is king, providing the perfect crisp balance to a slice of salty, sweet or smoky fish, followed closely by **red onion**. It is often lightly pickled and used as a garnish.

When it comes to **fruit**, nowadays like most places, the Nordic countries are well supplied with imports from countries far and wide. But if you're keeping things close to home, choose **berries** and **rhubarb** in the summer, with stone fruits, such as **cherries**, **plums** and **apricots** towards the end of this season. **Pears** and **apples** are found in abundance as we head into autumn.

Since olive trees don't take well to the Nordic landscape, **rapeseed oil** (or canola oil) is used instead, as well as butter. As well as being a local ingredient, rapeseed oil actually contains less saturated fat than either olive oil or butter.

Fruit and **malt vinegars** replace the balsamic vinegar or wine vinegars that we are used to in our predominantly classical European cooking styles. In Sweden they often use a very strong vinegar called **ättiksprit** in their pickling solution. Ättiksprit is an essence of vinegar and can be up to three times stronger in terms of its acidity than other vinegars; it has twelve per cent acidity. As a comparison, common apple and malt vinegars have only five per cent acidity.

Nordic mustard has a very different flavour profile from other mustards. They are much sweeter and always contain sugar. See page 43 or a classic Nordic mustard recipe (Finnish sweet mustard) and a Mustard dill sauce.

White pepper is preferred to black pepper and sugar somehow manages to find its way into many dishes.

The culture of open sandwiches all across the region (see pages 71–5) has resulted in an abundance of 'toppings'. **Liver paste**, **cured** or **smoked fish** and **meats** usually make up the base, on to which **fresh vegetables** and **cheese** are piled.

In most supermarkets you will find **sweet breads**, developed so that they keep well for the purpose of open sandwiches. **Dried breads** and, of course, **rye bread** are also very popular.

Food preservation

The Nordic region is no Mediterranean. With vigorous, contrasting seasons and long winter months, methods of food preservation were a necessity in days gone past. Brining, smoking, pickling and curing have left such a mark on the culture that even though they are no longer essential for survival, they are still popular today and are rightly celebrated at the new Nordic table.

Two fundamental themes running throughout all contemporary Nordic cooking are balance – in terms of both flavour and texture – and a reinvention of traditional techniques. Preserving food has both of these in abundance. From the acid-sharp crunch provided by a quickly pickled garnish, to the rich, silky smoked salmon that has come to be loved the world over, these historical skills provide dynamic flavour profiles and wonderful contrasting textures.

There are, of course, entire books written on each of these skills and on the following pages I have given you just a glimpse of what can be achieved. But, hopefully, these will enable you – often very simply – to add a taste of new Nordic to your cooking and encourage you to experiment in the kitchen.

Brining

I'm writing about brining ahead of the more obvious preservation techniques because, although it has taken a bit of a back seat in contemporary cooking, it has a lot of culinary value. The ubiquitously popular cold-smoked salmon is brined before it is smoked, and herring is brined before being pickled. Brining is a key stage in the production of some of the most famous Nordic foods.

Brining works by hydrating the tissue cells and its effects are three-fold: it seasons, tenderises and preserves. Below is a good recipe for brine, suitable for fish and seafood. Not all brines contain sugar, as it only partially penetrates the flesh, but I think it is worth using to balance the saltiness. A recommended brine for red meats and poultry is 250 ml (8½ fl oz/1 cup) of water to 1 tablespoon salt. (Sugar is less commonly used in brines for meats as it can make the meat watery if pan-frying or grilling, and the sugar can burn easily when cooking at a higher temperature.) Meat will need longer in the brine than fish, but timings will depend entirely on the weight and quality of the meat you use. As a very rough guide, a small cut (such as a chicken breast) will need 30 minutes–1 hour, whereas larger cuts (such as a whole turkey or a piece of pork belly) will need 12–24 hours. For longer brining times, use a non-metallic bowl to avoid tainting the flavour.

Brine for fish and seafood

MAKES ENOUGH FOR 800 G (1 LB 12 OZ) FISH OR SEAFOOD

1 LITRE (34 FL OZ) 4 CUPS WARM WATER

2 TABLESPOONS SALT

2 TABLESPOONS CASTER (SUPERFINE) SUGAR

Mix together all the ingredients in a bowl, stirring until the salt and sugar have dissolved.

Fully submerge the fish or seafood in the brine, weighting it down with a plate if necessary. Leave to brine according to these following guidelines:

Delicate trout, shellfish and sardines require as little as 15 minutes. More robust fish, such as salmon, herring, mackerel and swordfish, can be left for up to 40 minutes.

Make sure to pat the fish or seafood dry before cooking (unless you are poaching it).

DROTT-KAVIAR
EN NY KLASSIKER

Smoking

Today, smoking ingredients is still common practice in Nordic countries and the flavour typifies Nordic cuisine. Smokehouses are dotted all along the coastline and in new Nordic restaurants, you name it, it is smoked!

Typically, you will find smoked salmon, trout, eel, kipper, mackerel and shrimp. Less commonly, meat is smoked, and when it is, it is usually only venison, pork or chicken.

Smoking is a time-consuming process with a lot of variables and it can require a good deal of trial and error. With some basic knowledge though, a lot of fun can be had messing around with temperatures, duration and ingredients to achieve different results.

It is very common for Nordic summer holiday houses to have an outdoor smoker for the haul of fish or a bounty of game you might bring back after a day out, but in restaurants and the homes of those living in the city there is a vast range of more practical methods to add that wonderful smoky flavour to your food. Rather than cooking the food through entirely (as a conventional smoker often will), these domestic methods simply impart their smoke flavour before the food is properly cooked by other means. The best salmon fillet I have ever eaten was smoked first to impart flavour and then cooked in the oven afterwards. The lingering smoke flavour was delicious yet it had the consistency of a salmon fillet cooked normally.

On the following pages I've included those methods most suitable for the home cook. Read on for a guide to timings and how different woods can impart a range of flavours.

If you are going to experiment a little it is best to use a kitchen thermometer to check the internal temperatures of meats, particularly pork and chicken, to avoid running in to nasty incidents with bacteria.

Wood

The general rule is to use a hardwood and avoid wood from evergreens. Usually woodchips are recommended, but you can also use branches. People often get hung up on the type of wood to use and, although it does have some impact on the resulting flavour, it is not the most significant component of well-smoked food. It's the quality of the meat, fish or vegetables, the seasoning you use, the temperature and the fire control that are going to have the most effect on the taste. Once you have perfected the other elements, then play around with different woody flavours. Here are a few pointers:

Hickory chips

This is the most commonly used wood. It has a pungent, bacon-like flavour and is good for all smoking but be aware that it is quite strong. It works best with vegetables, pork, game and red meat.

Cherry, apple, beech chips or branches

These give a light, slightly sweet flavour that is good for poultry, all fish and seafood, cheeses and game.

Birch branches or chips

Like hickory, birch is quite strong so works best with robust ingredients like red meats, game and poultry.

Juniper branches

These are used in the final stages of smoking, once other woods have done most of the work, to impart a gin-like flavour. It works very well with seafood and vegetables.

Domestic smoking techniques

The techniques outlined here are suitable for small-scale smoking – 300 g (10½ oz) up to 2 kg (4 lb 6 oz) of meat, fish or vegetables. Anything larger should really be attempted in a standard smoker.

Smoking gun

This hand-held device offers an alternative to traditional smoking techniques. Already-cooked vegetables, sauces or raw foods can be flavoured with this tool and then stored in sealable bags or containers. Guides to cooking techniques and times are supplied with the product.

Closed gas barbecue

This uses a standard lidded gas barbecue. Soak 2 handfuls of woodchips in water for 15 minutes. Drain and spread them out in a small disposable aluminium tray. Place the tray on one corner of the grill-rack, directly over the flame bars or lava rocks.

Heat the grill to high for about 15–20 minutes with the lid on. Turn off the middle burners and place the food over them to smoke.

Kettle barbecue

Soak two handfuls of woodchips in water for 15 minutes. Drain, then combine with the coal and pile up on one side of the barbecue. Place a small disposable aluminium tray filled with water on the grill-rack directly above the coals and chips.

Light the coals and let them burn for 15 minutes, or until the internal temperature is at least 120°C (250°F). Set the food on the other side of the grill-rack, above the empty space, and close the lid, making sure the ventilation holes in the lid sit directly above the food and that they are fully open.

In the oven

If you are not the outdoor type or you don't have a garden, you can still experiment with smoking your own food. Using a barbecue is preferable, though, mainly because your house could get full of smoke!

Preheat the oven to 120°C (250°F). Soak one large handful of woodchips in water for 15 minutes. Spread them out in a large disposable aluminium tray in a single layer. Position a wire rack directly above the chips (it should be about the same size as the tray). Pour enough water into the tray to form a very shallow film over the bottom.

Place the food on the wire rack. Using the thickest foil you can find, form a tent that peaks well above the food, giving the smoke room to move around inside.

Ensure the foil is sealed around the edges of the tray so the smoke can't escape. Place on the bottom shelf of the oven and smoke away!

During the smoking process, the water may evaporate and dry out your chips and also your food. For longer timings (which I recommend doing outside if you can) you will need to keep it topped up. This is when your kitchen will fill with smoke. Remove the tray from the oven and, with your outside door open, lift a small edge of the foil to peek in and check. If it looks like it's drying out, pour some more water into the tray, re-wetting the chips and re-creating the film of water at the bottom. Cover up with foil again and return to the oven.

A guide to smoking times & temperatures

If you are using one of the domestic techniques described above to impart some lovely smoky flavour, I would recommend smoking your meat, fish, seafood and vegetables for 20–40 minutes, and then finish cooking them using conventional methods. Bear in mind that the smoke will have very gently cooked the food, especially delicate fish and seafood and thinly sliced meats, so it may not need cooking for very long afterwards. To concentrate the flavour, you can trap some of the smoke with the food in a well-sealed container and refrigerate for a little while to allow the flavours to develop before cooking.

The guidelines below are for conventional smoking, which cooks the food as well as imparting flavour.

FISH & SEAFOOD

Hot-smoked fish

This works well with salmon, trout and other oily fish, such as mackerel and tuna.

Temperature: 65°C (150°F)

Length: 6 hours for a large fillet

Cold-smoked salmon, swordfish, tuna, ocean trout

Temperature: Air temperature no higher than 33°C (91°F) to avoid actually cooking the flesh. Since the temperature is so low, it isn't really possible to cold-smoke salmon at home.

Length: 12–16 hours

PRAWNS (SHRIMP)

The following technique is for tiger prawns or similar. Small prawns will need half the time. Before smoking prawns, salt them and let them sit for 30 minutes, then rinse them well. Place in the smoker for 10 minutes then turn them over. They will be ready when they are completely opaque all over. This should not take longer than 15–20 minutes. Eat them immediately or chill them.

CHEESE

The key to smoking cheese is to keep the temperature low, around 30°C (86°F).

With this in mind, smoking outside in colder weather is ideal. Any cheese is suitable. Cut it into 10 cm x 10 cm x 1 cm (4 in x 4 in x ½ in) pieces and smoke it for 3 hours. Adjust this time for the next occasion according to your personal taste. To store the cheese, wrap each piece in plastic wrap and keep in the refrigerator. Ideally, you want to wait a week or two to allow the flavours to develop.

MEAT

Beef or venison

For a 2 kg (4 lb 6 oz) brisket

Temperature: 110°C (230°F)

Length: 6–7 hours

Chicken

For a whole chicken

Temperature: 120°C (250°F)

Length: 4 hours

For 1 kg (2 lb 3 oz) boneless, skinless chicken breasts

Temperature: 120°C (250°F)

Length: 1½–2 hours. Use a meat thermometer to check that the internal temperature of the chicken reaches at least 70°C (160°F) to be safe.

VEGETABLES

Roasted vegetables can benefit from a little smoke flavour but it's best to use a smoking gun to impart flavour once they are cooked rather than cook them in a smoker.

Using smoke to cook vegetables is most effective on permeable vegetables, like halved onions, tomatoes and cabbage wedges. It is possible to smoke potatoes or beetroot (beets), but it is very time consuming and not really worth the effort.

Pickling

The process of pickling in vinegar is an age-old technique traditionally used to preserve vegetables and fish. Today, we are attracted more to the flavour and texture that pickling brings to dishes than its practical uses in storing food. Still, we should not discount its original benefits. If you're at a farmers' market and there's a particularly glorious vegetable in abundance, buy it in bulk and pickle it. Later in the year you can enjoy travelling back in time via your taste buds.

Nordic folk are by no means opposed to some sweetness in their food, and the acidity from the vinegar in pickles plays an important role in balancing those flavours. The dishes in this book are often garnished with a vegetable that has been lightly pickled for this purpose. They also add a satisfying crunch and are very attractive to the eye.

Some pickling tips

- Avoid using metallic or reactive materials when pickling as they can affect the flavour. Use ceramic or glass.
- Non-iodised salt helps prevent the pickling solution from becoming cloudy.
- The best vegetables for pickling are those that have a low starch content. Vegetables with higher levels need longer in pickling brine – at least a week. Cauliflower, carrots, beetroot (beets) and cabbage all pickle well and will keep in a lidded jar in the refrigerator for up to a month.
- How thinly you slice your vegetables will determine how long they need in the pickling solution. Don't leave them for too long; the ideal is a sharp, fresh crunchy vegetable that rounds off a dish and balances any sweeter flavours.
- Vegetables with a high water content break down quickly if sliced thinly, so they only require brief pickling.
- Traditionally, recipes may call for pre-boiling or curing and then rinsing vegetables before pickling, but if you slice them thinly enough you won't need to.
- Try to use organic or farm fresh produce and always give it a thorough rinse.
- Pickling fish is a classic technique in Nordic cooking and for those willing to endure the process it is very rewarding. Pre-cured fillets of small oily fish, such as sardines, mackerel and herring respond the most effectively. The fish will need to be soaked in water for 24 hours, rinsing occasionally, to remove the salt, then they should be pickled for at least 24 hours. The sweeter, light pickling solution (see page 34) is best for this. Pickling raw, or unsalted fish is a much lengthier process, taking at least 5 days.

Vinegars

The vinegars that best complement Nordic cuisine are malt, apple and basic white. It is unusual to see vinegars from other parts of Europe being used, such as balsamic and wine vinegars. A good pickling solution using a regular vinegar would be 1 part water to 1 part vinegar.

Spices

Almost any combination of spices can be used to flavour your pickling solution but I find the best use common Nordic ingredients. Be careful with cloves and allspice berries though, as they can be overpowering. Some of my favourites are:

— Allspice berries
— Bay leaves
— Celery seeds
— Cloves
— Dill seeds
— Fennel seeds
— Juniper berries
— Mustard seeds
— Star anise

Light pickling solution

This is a sweet solution with a distinct flavour from the juniper berries. It is a good pickling solution for delicate vegetables or for those that require less pickling time, such as those with a higher water content. Red onion, fennel or radish are all good options. As a general rule, this solution is suitable for vegetables that can be eaten raw. For vegetables that you would rarely eat raw, I suggest using the sharper, stronger solution below.

MAKES ENOUGH SOLUTION FOR 500 G–900 G (1 LB 2 OZ–2 LB) VEGETABLES

- 250 ML (8½ FL OZ/1 CUP) APPLE CIDER VINEGAR
- 250 ML (8½ FL OZ/1 CUP) COLD WATER
- 150 G (5½ OZ) CASTER (SUPERFINE) SUGAR
- 1 TEASPOON NON-IODISED SALT
- 3 JUNIPER BERRIES
- 2 ALLSPICE BERRIES
- 2 BAY LEAVES

Thinly slice the ingredient you are going to pickle (preferably with a mandoline) and set aside in a non-reactive bowl.

Bring all the pickling solution ingredients to the boil in a saucepan then reduce the heat and simmer gently, stirring, for 2 minutes, until all the sugar has dissolved.

Allow to cool, then pour over the ingredient you are pickling.

Heavy pickling solution

This sharp acidic solution is great for vegetables that you would normally cook before eating. Denser vegetables, such as baby onions, garlic cloves or root vegetables will all work well. Thinly sliced raw beetroot (beet) is another great option; leave it in the solution for 1–2 days. Use non-iodised salt so the solution doesn't turn cloudy.

MAKES ENOUGH SOLUTION FOR 500 G–900 G (1 LB 2 OZ–2 LB) VEGETABLES

- 1 TABLESPOON MUSTARD SEEDS, PREFERABLY BROWN
- 1 TEASPOON DILL SEEDS
- 300 ML (10 FL OZ) WHITE VINEGAR
- 200 ML (7 FL OZ) WATER
- 70 G (2½ OZ) CASTER (SUPERFINE) SUGAR
- 2 TABLESPOONS NON-IODISED SALT
- 1 BAY LEAF

Dry-fry the mustard and dill seeds in a small saucepan over a medium heat for about 2 minutes, or until fragrant.

Add the remaining ingredients and stir until the sugar and salt have dissolved. Bring to the boil then immediately remove from the heat.

Allow to cool, then pour over the ingredient you are pickling.

Curing

Curing uses the process of osmosis, in which a mixture of sugar and salt work together to very lightly 'cook' the food. The flavour is uniquely sweet and salty. In new Nordic cooking it is most commonly used for seafood, particularly salmon, but you can also cure vegetables that have strong flavours, such as onion. Unlike in southern European countries, cured meats are not very common in Nordic regions.

You can combine any spice you like with the salt and sugar to impart specific flavours into the fish, vegetables and meats.

Gravlax is probably the most famous Nordic example of curing. *Grav* means grave and *lax* means salmon because, traditionally, fishermen buried whole fish in the sand, and left it to lightly ferment. It was a great way to preserve excess stock for the future when the catch may not be so abundant. Nowadays, salmon is cured in a more conventional manner, but the name has stuck. In the recipe below, I use juniper berries and mustard seeds, which give the salmon a nice gin-like flavour.

Gravlax, juniper & mustard seeds

Cucumber, horseradish, fresh dill, potatoes, bread and egg (in any form) make great accompaniments to gravlax.

SERVES 8

1 TABLESPOON MUSTARD SEEDS, PREFERABLY YELLOW

4 DRIED JUNIPER BERRIES

125 G (4½ OZ/½ CUP) CASTER (SUPERFINE) SUGAR

80 G (2¾ OZ/⅓ CUP) SALT

1 X 1 KG (2 LB 3 OZ) SALMON FILLET, SKIN ON

Dry-fry the mustard seeds and juniper berries in a small pan over a medium heat for 1–2 minutes, until they begin to pop. Tip on to a plate and leave to cool, then crush using a mortar and pestle. Stir through the sugar and salt.

Line a ceramic dish with plastic wrap leaving plenty of overhang. Place the fish on top, skin side down.

Pour the salt mixture over the fish and evenly distribute it so it is well covered, patting it down into the flesh. Flip the fillet over as neatly as possible and rearrange the salt mixture underneath if necessary.

Cover with the plastic wrap and weigh down using small plates or food tins. Chill in the refrigerator for 2 days, flipping it over at least twice.

To serve, first drain off any liquid and wipe the fillet clean. Cut across the fillet on a slight angle to produce thin strips.

CHAPTER TWO

Larder

Nordic culinary tradition is very much based on necessity. In such a harsh and challenging climate and terrain, there used to be a very real need to preserve and store food just in order to survive through the long winter months.

Eating fresh berries was a very brief luxury during the height of summer; most were made into jams. Vegetables were pickled. Potatoes and root vegetables were stored in the cellar. Even breads were very thin so that they could be dried and packed away. Milk was turned into soured or curdled milk, or sour cream, or sometimes cheese. Butter and eggs were real luxuries, hard to come by and often traded for more essential ingredients.

Although times have changed and food from all around the world is now more easily sourced from supermarkets, this long history has heavily influenced the refrigerators, store cupboards and menus of the modern Nordic kitchen.

This chapter contains a collection of recipes for light meals and snacks that make use of these traditional pantry staples. In the new Nordic style, they celebrate contemporary techniques and preparation methods while holding firm to the region's history and tradition – where new meets old.

Mustard dill sauce

This sauce is very versatile but it is especially great with potatoes, herring or smoked salmon. In the seafood chapter it is served with the Mackerel, buckwheat and pear salad (see page 137).

MAKES ENOUGH TO FILL 1 X 300 G (10½ OZ) JAR

- 3 TABLESPOONS WHOLEGRAIN MUSTARD
- 2 TEASPOONS WHITE WINE VINEGAR
- 1 EGG YOLK
- 1 TABLESPOON CASTER (SUPERFINE) SUGAR
- PINCH OF WHITE PEPPER
- 200 ML (7 FL OZ) SUNFLOWER OIL
- 60 G (2 OZ) DILL, CHOPPED

Sterilise a glass jar by washing it thoroughly in hot soapy water, rinsing well, then putting it on a baking tray in a low oven (120°C/250°F) for 20 minutes. Leave to cool.

Mix together the mustard, vinegar, egg yolk, sugar, white pepper and a pinch of salt.

Add the oil in a thin stream, whisking vigorously, until completely incorporated and emulsified. Finally, stir through the dill.

Transfer to the sterilised jar and store in the refrigerator for up to one week.

Finnish sweet mustard (left)

Nordic mustards are incredibly sweet, and most have a consistency that can be likened to thick honey. To balance out some of the sweetness, mustard powder is more often used over mustard seeds as it has a more intense flavour.

MAKES ENOUGH TO FILL 1 X 350 G (11½ OZ) JAR

- 5 TABLESPOONS HOT DRY MUSTARD POWDER, SUCH AS COLMAN'S ENGLISH MUSTARD OR KEEN'S MUSTARD
- 125 G (4½ OZ/½ CUP) CASTER (SUPERFINE) SUGAR
- 1 TEASPOON TABLE SALT
- 250 ML (8½ FL OZ/1 CUP) POURING (SINGLE/LIGHT) CREAM
- 1 TABLESPOON RAPESEED OIL
- 2 TABLESPOONS APPLE CIDER VINEGAR
- JUICE OF ½ LEMON

Sterilise a glass jar by washing it thoroughly in hot soapy water, rinsing well, then putting it on a baking tray in a low oven (120°C/250°F) for 20 minutes. Leave to cool.

In a bowl, thoroughly combine the mustard powder, sugar and salt with the back of a spoon.

Tip into a saucepan set over a low heat. A tablespoon at a time, add the cream, incorporating each spoonful before adding the next. Stir in the remaining ingredients and bring to the boil, stirring all the time. Simmer for 7–8 minutes, stirring often, until the mixture thickens and darkens slightly.

Remove from the heat and leave to cool before transferring to the sterilised jar. This mustard will keep in the refrigerator for several weeks.

Brown butter

The many different uses for and types of butter are notable in Nordic cuisine. In cafés and bistros, butter is often served whipped, giving it a light, airy consistency not dissimilar to whipped cream. The contrast it makes with crunchy crispbreads is very satisfying. Try it out by simply whipping some up with an electric beater. Use room-temperature butter; it will take about 5 minutes.

Also common in cooking or to spread on bread is brown butter. Known more popularly worldwide as beurre noisette, it has a lovely nutty, caramel flavour that brings an additional depth of flavour to dishes. This recipe shows you how to make basic brown butter, and then I add extra butter for a spreadable version, suitable for the table. On page 292 you will find a recipe for brown butter ice cream.

I also recommend adding a little spice to this recipe. Half a teaspoon of lightly ground fennel seeds, dill seeds or parsley seeds can be cooked with the butter.

MAKES 500 G (1 LB 2 OZ)

200 G SALTED BUTTER PLUS 300 G (10½ OZ) EXTRA IF MAKING THE SPREADABLE VERSION

Dice the butter and, if making the spreadable version, leave the 300 g (10½ oz) amount in a bowl at room temperature.

In a small saucepan set over a medium heat cook the 200 g (7 oz) butter, until it starts to colour a light brown. This will take about 2–3 minutes depending on what type of pan you are using.

Immediately remove the pan from the heat and transfer it to a cold surface to stop the cooking. A marble or stone surface is ideal for this; otherwise use a chopping board or tea towel. It will keep cooking after you have removed it from the heat, so make sure you transfer it before it gets too dark. You will know immediately if you have burnt it or have taken it too far on the heat as it won't smell so sweet and you are likely to detect a smoky bitterness. The butter is now ready to be used in your cooking or added to other dishes.

To make the spreadable version, pour into a separate bowl and place in the refrigerator for about 15 minutes, until it has almost set.

Remove from refrigerator and blend into the reserved room-temperature butter. Whip them together if you prefer a lighter spread. Serve spread on bread or crispbreads.

G.FELIX.SOLINGEN
GLORIAWERK
RUSTFRI
STAAL

Rhubarb chutney

The natural tartness of rhubarb makes it the perfect candidate for preserving with sugar and vinegar.

MAKES ENOUGH TO FILL 2 X 300 G (10½ OZ) JARS

- 4 RHUBARB STALKS, CHOPPED INTO 2 CM (¾ IN) DICE
- 3 TABLESPOONS CASTER (SUPERFINE) SUGAR
- ½ TEASPOON SALT
- 1 ONION, FINELY DICED
- 1 TABLESPOON RAPESEED OIL
- 2 TEASPOONS MUSTARD SEEDS
- 1 TABLESPOON APPLE CIDER VINEGAR

Sterilise the glass jars by washing them thoroughly in hot soapy water, rinsing well, then putting them on a baking tray in a low oven (120°C/250°F) for 20 minutes. Leave to cool.

Toss the chopped rhubarb in the sugar and the salt.

Gently fry the onion in the oil over a medium heat for 5 minutes, until soft and translucent.

Add the mustard seeds and when they start to pop stir in the rhubarb and vinegar. Cover with a lid and cook for 5 minutes, until the rhubarb softens and collapses. Remove the lid and cook for a further 7 minutes, stirring occasionally. Set aside to cool.

Transfer to the sterilised jars and keep in the refrigerator for up to a week.

Plum, vanilla & rosemary jam

This is a great jam recipe which, unlike almost all jams, doesn't feature any sugar. The prunes give it a lovely deep flavour reminiscent of dried fruit, while the sweetness comes from the ripeness of the plums. If your plums aren't quite ripe enough the jam can end up tart, but don't despair – like this it makes a delicious sharp spread paired with savoury ingredients such as cheese or meat.

MAKES 3 X 400 G (14 OZ) JARS

2 KG (4 LB 8 OZ) OVER-RIPE PLUMS, WASHED (BLACK OR AMBER PLUMS ARE PERFECT FOR THIS)

2 ROSEMARY STALKS

1 VANILLA BEAN, SPLIT LENGTHWAYS AND SEEDS SCRAPED

250 G (9 OZ) DRIED PITTED PRUNES, ROUGHLY CHOPPED

Preheat the oven to 100°C (200°F). Sterilise the glass jars by washing them thoroughly in soapy water, rinsing well, then putting them on a baking tray in the oven for 20 minutes. Leave to cool.

Halve the plums, keeping the stones in, and add to a large heavy-based saucepan together with the rosemary, split vanilla bean and seeds and prunes. Cook over a low heat for 2 hours, stirring occasionally to prevent the mixture sticking to the bottom of the pan. Remove the plum stones (these can be rinsed and kept to flavour vinegars) and continue to cook, stirring regularly, for a further 1½ hours, until you have a sticky, deep-red jam. Towards the end of this time the jam will be wanting to stick to the bottom of the pan, so keep an eye on it and be sure to keep stirring to make sure this doesn't happen.

Once cooked, leave the jam to cool, then spoon it into the sterilised jars. The jam will keep for up to 3 months – to keep it for longer, freeze it in a suitable container and defrost it when needed.

Ymer, ymerdrys & berries

Ymer *is Denmark's version of sour milk, but in this recipe you can use natural yoghurt instead. It is sprinkled with* ymerdrys, *a crunchy sweet topping made from Danish rye bread (see pages 231–233). As it is such an essential component of this recipe, make sure to use an authentic rye bread here, not a light, fluffy version. It must be heavy, waxy and dense. The bread's malty and sweet taste is a perfect complement to the slightly sour* ymer *or yoghurt.* Ymerdrys *is also a great garnish for savoury dishes, introducing a welcome sweetness; try it with the cod and parsnip recipe on page 134.*

SERVES 4–6

200 G (7 OZ) AUTHENTIC DANISH RYE BREAD (SEE PAGES 231–33), BROKEN INTO LARGE CHUNKS

2 TABLESPOONS BROWN SUGAR

600 G (1 LB 5 OZ) YMER OR NATURAL YOGHURT

400 G (14 OZ) MIXED FRESH BERRIES

Preheat the oven to 180°C (350°F). Pulse the bread in a food processor, gradually adding the sugar, until the consistency resembles loose soil.

Tip the mixture on to a baking tray lined with baking paper and cook in the oven for 10–15 minutes, so it takes on a rich brown colour. Watch closely in the last 5 minutes to make sure it doesn't burn. Remove from the oven and allow to cool on the tray.

Enjoy sprinkled on top of ymer or yoghurt with some fresh berries.

Buckwheat porridge, apple & ginger

Apples and pears are very well loved in Scandinavian cuisine and trees are everywhere, in orchards or lining major thoroughfares, beautifully old and gnarled with twisted trunks.

A friend made a fantastic short film about preparing this dish using apples picked in the garden surrounding her house. In this recipe, the contrast of the earthy buckwheat with the zingy ginger, lemon and tart apple is fantastic – a great alternative to regular porridge.

SERVES 4

200 G (7 OZ) CRUSHED/CRACKED BUCKWHEAT

2 TABLESPOONS LINSEEDS (FLAX SEEDS)

1 TEASPOON GROUND CINNAMON

2 GRANNY SMITH APPLES OR ANOTHER TART VARIETY

2 CM (¾ IN) PIECE FRESH GINGER, PEELED

JUICE OF ½ LEMON

1 TABLESPOON HONEY

MILK OR PLANT-BASED MILK, TO SERVE

Bring the buckwheat, linseed, cinnamon and 500 ml (17 fl oz/2 cups) water to a simmer in a saucepan over a medium heat. Cook for about 5 minutes, stirring to start with, then simmer with the lid on for a further 5 minutes. Remove from the heat and allow to sit, still with the lid on, for 10 minutes.

Grate the apples and ginger into a bowl and stir through the lemon juice and honey.

Divide the buckwheat between bowls and top with the grated apple and ginger mixture. Serve with milk or plant-based milks.

Radish, butter & honey

A crisp, refreshing radish eaten on its own, or dipped in a little salt, is one of nature's simple pleasures. But paired with sweet honey and this salty, spiced butter it makes for a real treat.

SERVES 2-3

1 TEASPOON CELERY SEEDS OR FENNEL SEEDS

1 TABLESPOON SEA SALT FLAKES, PLUS EXTRA TO SERVE

100 G (3½ OZ) UNSALTED BUTTER, AT ROOM TEMPERATURE

400 G (14 OZ) FRESH RADISHES

80 ML (2½ FL OZ/⅓ CUP) HONEY

Lightly toast the seeds in a non-stick frying pan over a low heat for a couple of minutes, until they have darkened in colour and give off a nutty fragrance. Remove from the heat and grind with the salt using a mortar and pestle. Combine with the butter in a small bowl.

Serve the radishes with the butter and honey for dipping and sprinkle with a little extra salt.

Rare beef, parsnip chips & grated egg

Boiled eggs are very well loved in all Nordic countries. No home is without an egg slicer (see page 16) and sliced eggs adorn open sandwiches every morning, usually topped with fish roe or a creamy rora, such as gubbröra *or* skagenröra *(see page 79). In this recipe, the egg is grated and serves to soften the mustard sauce which in turn perfectly complements the rich beef. Parsnips are used as much for their extra-crunchy texture as for their unique, sweet flavour. A simple and delicious dish to serve cold on a hot day.*

SERVES 4

1 X 500 G (1 LB 2 OZ) WHOLE PIECE OF BEEF (RIB, SIRLOIN OR FILLET)

1 TABLESPOON RAPESEED OIL

2 EGGS

1 PARSNIP

300 ML (10 FL OZ) SUNFLOWER OIL

MUSTARD DILL SAUCE (SEE PAGE 43), FOR DRIZZLING

Preheat the oven to 180°C (350°F). In a frying pan over a high heat, cook the beef in the rapeseed oil for a minute or so on all sides, just to brown the meat and seal it. Transfer to a roasting tray and cook in the oven for 15–20 minutes. You want it to be quite rare so it should still be quite soft to the touch. Remove from the oven and leave to rest for at least 10 minutes, before chilling in the refrigerator for a minimum of 2 hours.

Boil the eggs for 7–8 minutes until hard-boiled. Cool under running water and leave in a bowl of cold water for at least 5 minutes.

Meanwhile, using a mandoline or vegetable peeler, slice the parsnips into very thin discs.

In a heavy-based frying pan, heat the sunflower oil to 180°C (350°F). If you don't have a thermometer, you can check the oil is hot enough by dropping in one of the parsnip slices: if it sizzles and floats to the top, it's ready to go. Fry the parsnip slices for a minute or so, until they turn golden brown. Using a slotted spoon, transfer them to some paper towel to drain.

Slice the beef thinly across the grain and arrange on serving plates. Peel the egg and then grate it over the top. Scatter with the parsnip chips and drizzle with the mustard dill sauce.

Pâté, fennel jam & hazelnuts

Liver paste (known commonly as pâté) is a popular topping for the ubiquitous open sandwiches found all across the Nordic region. Unfortunately, it is usually mass-produced and packed with additives and preservatives. Chicken livers are cheap and delicious, and cooked, as here, with spiced aquavit they provide a little Nordic twist on the southern European classic. This is a great grazer served on crispbread, with sweetness from the fennel jam and an earthy crunch from the nuts.

SERVES 8

300 G (10½ OZ) SALTED BUTTER, AT ROOM TEMPERATURE

2 SHALLOTS, FINELY CHOPPED

1 GARLIC CLOVE, FINELY CHOPPED

2 TEASPOONS RAPESEED OIL

400 G (14 OZ) WHOLE CHICKEN LIVERS, AFTER TRIMMING

SEA SALT

WHITE PEPPER

60 ML (2 FL OZ/¼ CUP) SPICED AQUAVIT (SEE PAGE 296)

A FEW THYME SPRIGS, LEAVES PICKED, PLUS EXTRA TO GARNISH

RYE BREAD (SEE PAGES 231–33) OR CRISPBREADS, TO SERVE

100 G (3½ OZ) TOASTED HAZELNUTS, ROUGHLY CHOPPED

FENNEL JAM

½ TEASPOON SALT

1 X 600 G (1 LB 5 OZ) FENNEL BULB (OR 2 SMALLER ONES), VERY THINLY SLICED (USING A MANDOLINE IF YOU HAVE ONE)

140 G (5 OZ) CASTER (SUPERFINE) SUGAR

JUICE OF ½ LEMON

Sterilise a couple of glass jars by washing them thoroughly in hot soapy water, rinsing well, then putting them on a baking tray in a low oven (120°C/250°F) for 20 minutes. Leave to cool.

To make the fennel jam, combine the salt, fennel, sugar and lemon juice in a small heavy-based saucepan over a very low heat and cook for at least 40 minutes and up to an hour, stirring often to make sure it doesn't catch on the base of the pan. The fennel should be soft and the mixture a rich golden colour. If the mixture starts to dry out, cover with a lid. Allow to cool a little then transfer the jam to the sterilised jars (they can be stored in the refrigerator for several weeks).

Meanwhile, clarify 100 g (3½ oz) of the butter by melting it in a small saucepan over a low heat until the white solids separate out. Gently pour the golden melted butter into a bowl or jug and discard the solids.

In a non-stick frying pan sauté the shallots and garlic in the oil over a medium heat for 3 minutes, or until soft. Increase the heat, add the chicken livers and season with sea salt and a pinch of white pepper. Cook the livers on all sides for a minute or so, just to seal, then continue to cook for 4–5 minutes, until they start to give out some moisture. Pour in the aquavit, cook for 1 minute more, then transfer to a blender.

Add the remaining butter, some more white pepper and the thyme leaves and blend for 3 minutes, stopping every so often to scrape down the sides.

Transfer to a shallow 600 ml (20½ fl oz) glass or ceramic dish. If you want a very smooth pâté, pass the mixture through a fine sieve straight into the dish. Pour over the clarified butter then set in the refrigerator for at least 2 hours. The flavours develop with time, so ideally leave it overnight. Covered in plastic wrap, it will keep for up to a week.

Serve the pâté with rye bread or crispbreads and the fennel jam. Scatter over the toasted hazelnuts and garnish with the extra thyme leaves.

Elderflower cordial

At Nordic latitudes, the seasons are intense. Those who live in this hard and ever-changing landscape learn to recognise the early clues that hint at the warmer weather and to know what grows when and where so as not to miss out. This far north, elderflowers can bloom for as little as two short weeks in late spring, making them all the more special and worthy of being celebrated. Elsewhere in the world they can flower well into June. This delicious cordial can be diluted with sparkling or still mineral water or used to flavour sweet dishes, such as sorbets, creams and cakes. And it stores very well. It is well worth hunting down a supply and climbing a ladder into the trees.

Both the flowers and berries have a wide array of culinary uses. The berries, which come later in the year, are poisonous if eaten raw (as are the roots, bark and leaves) but they can be cooked into syrups or jams. The flowers can also be covered in batter and made into fritters, or they can be dried to make tea. If you're not certain of what is edible and what is not, make sure you take someone with you who knows.

Flavoured waters are very popular during the summer months in Nordic countries. Slices of lemon, orange, cucumber or fresh berries and herbs are the most common flavourings. I suggest serving this elderflower cordial with a slice of lemon or a few ribbons of cucumber.

MAKES 1.5 LITRES (51 FL OZ/6 CUPS)

1 KG (2 LB 3 OZ) CASTER (SUPERFINE) SUGAR

1.5 LITRES (51 FL OZ/6 CUPS) BOILING WATER

4 LEMONS, WASHED

20 G (¾ OZ) CITRIC ACID

30 LARGE ELDERFLOWER FLOWER HEADS, SHAKEN TO REMOVE ANY INSECTS

Place the sugar in a large saucepan, stockpot or non-metallic bowl. Pour the boiling water over the top and stir until all the sugar has dissolved. Leave to cool to room temperature.

Finely grate the zest of the lemons into the sugar water, then thickly slice the lemons and add them as well.

Stir in the citric acid, then submerge the flower heads in the mixture and stir again. Cover with a clean tea towel (dish towel) and leave to steep for 48 hours at room temperature.

Sterilise a couple of 750 ml (25½ fl oz/3 cup) glass bottles, by washing them thoroughly in hot soapy water, rinsing well, then putting them on a baking tray in a low oven (120°C/250°F) for 20 minutes. Leave to cool.

Strain the cordial through some fine muslin (cheesecloth) into a clean bowl. Using a funnel, pour the strained liquid into sterilised bottles then seal and store in a cool, dark place (not the refrigerator). You can drink it straightaway and it will keep for a few weeks. Alternatively, freeze in plastic bottles for up to a year. Depending on how sweet your tooth is and the intensity of the flowers, I recommend diluting it 1 part cordial to 4 parts water.

Fermented brussels sprouts

Fermenting is a preservation method that has been used in Nordic countries since the time of the Vikings and a worthwhile endeavour, particularly given it also produces alcohol and vinegar. For some it may be hard to differentiate between a pickled cabbage and a fermented one but the difference is there and it's a beautiful thing.

MAKES 3 X 400 G (14 OZ) JARS

1 KG (2 LB 4 OZ) BRUSSELS SPROUTS

35 G (1¼ OZ) SEA SALT

1 GARLIC CLOVE, GRATED

1 TABLESPOON GRATED FRESH GINGER

1 TABLESPOON RAW (DEMERARA) SUGAR

1 TEASPOON WHITE PEPPER

1 TEASPOON MUSTARD SEEDS

4 SPRING ONIONS (SCALLIONS), GREEN PARTS ONLY, TRIMMED AND CUT INTO 2 CM (¾ IN) PIECES

500 ML (18 FL OZ/2 CUPS) MINERAL WATER

Preheat the oven to 100°C (200°F). Sterilise the glass jars by washing them thoroughly in soapy water, rinsing well, then putting them on a baking tray in the oven for 20 minutes. Leave to cool.

Cut each brussels sprout into four thin discs. Combine the brussels sprout pieces and salt in a large bowl. Using your hands, massage the salt into the sprout pieces until they start to soften, then pour over enough tap water to cover. Place a plate over the sprout mixture and weigh it down with something heavy like a jar or food tin and leave to stand for 1–2 hours (this will help soften the sprouts and extract any bitterness).

Rinse and drain the sprouts. Rinse the sprouts under cold water three times and then soak again for 15–20 minutes.

In a large bowl, mix together the garlic, ginger and sugar to form a smooth paste. Stir in the spices. Add the spring onions and mineral water to the paste and use your hands to mix and coat everything thoroughly (you can wear gloves here if you like).

Pack the brussels sprouts into the jars, pressing it down with a spoon until the brine rises to fully submerge the vegetables, leaving at least 2.5 cm (1 in) of headspace between the sprouts and the top of the jars. Seal the jars with the lids.

Leave the jars at room temperature to ferment for 1–5 days. Check them daily to release any gases and press down on the vegetables with a clean finger or spoon to keep them submerged under the brine. Taste a little at this point, too! When the kimchi tastes ripe enough for your liking, transfer the jars to the refrigerator. You can eat it right away, but it's best after another week or two.

CHAPTER THREE

Classics

Winborgs
12%

Like many other culinary traditions, Nordic gastronomy has a long history of borrowing and adapting elements from abroad. However, there are distinct characteristics that set it apart. For instance, white pepper is often favoured over black; a choice likely influenced by ancient trade routes. The cuisine also features unique contrasts of sweet and sour flavours, achieved through skilful pairings of vinegars and sugars. Yet many beloved Nordic home-cooked meals and worker's lunches bear a heavy influence from classic European styles. Creamy, buttery sauces paired with meats and vegetables, for example, owe much to traditional French techniques.

Until not so long ago, most people's exposure to Nordic cuisine might have come from a trip to the large, ubiquitous Swedish furniture store, known for its traditional Swedish ingredients and ready-made food products – or through a friend-of-a-friend with Scandinavian roots. But this narrow lens hardly does justice to the depth and diversity of Nordic food culture! Today's modern Nordic cuisine embraces innovation, combining ancient methods with contemporary techniques to make the most of local, seasonal ingredients. The result? Dishes that are both exciting and unprecedented.

Still, the foundation of this culinary evolution lies in the classics. These dishes – simple, hearty, and incredibly nourishing – have earned their place as staples for good reason. While they may not rival stone-baked pizzas or exotic stir-fries on the world's stage, when prepared with care, these time-tested recipes truly shine and deserve to be celebrated.

In this chapter, you'll find recipes for these enduring favorites – dishes that form the backbone of Nordic cooking and continue to delight, generation after generation.

The Open Sandwich

When most people picture a smörgåsbord they imagine a huge table piled high with an abundance of hot and cold delicacies. But, its direct translation is actually 'sandwich table': an offering of sandwiches. And in Nordic countries these are open sandwiches, smørrebrød, rather than fillings held between two slices of bread. It is a true testament to the sandwich table's prominence in Nordic food culture that the word is known throughout the world.

In the morning, generally only butter is spread on slices of bread before being topped with your choice of ingredients, but as the day progresses a range of condiments come into play (see pages 73–5 for a few of my favourites). Nordic folk do not limit themselves to toast and jam with their juice and coffee though. You're more likely to find sliced deli meats, tinned fish, fish roe, even cheese in tubes! All sorts of crazy items. The best description I have come across of smørrebrød is 'emptying the entire refrigerator on to the table for breakfast'.

Cheese and cucumber are obligatory, set alongside hams, salamis, liver pastes, sliced eggs, sliced tomato, capsicum (bell pepper) and sprigs of fresh parsley and dill. Pickles are particularly popular in Denmark where the open sandwich culture is a way of life. The strict use of Danish rye bread for all smørrebrød, and the many smørrebrød-only eateries around the country has crowned Denmark the king of the open sandwich culture.

Although it is traditional to use rye bread (see pages 231–5) for the base of these sandwiches, you could also use soft or crisp *tunnbröd* (see page 224), sourdough, sunflower-seed breads and sweeter breads such as carrot and lingonberry.

The following pages include some of my most-loved toppings.

Smørrebrød

Open sandwiches are ubiquitously popular throughout all Nordic countries, being the go-to for a quick bite or speedy lunch. But it is Denmark that has a particular love for these rye bread-based snacks and they are the true heroes of Danish cuisine.

The most common topping is meat or fish in a creamy sauce of some variety, with a kick of acidity, usually from a pickle, and finished with a garnish – traditionally, dill or parsley. Like any sandwiches though, the flavour combinations are endless. Be generous with your toppings; consider them more of a salad that happens to have bread underneath, rather than a regular sandwich. Two good recipes for Danish rye bread can be found on pages 231–33.

ALL RECIPES MAKE 4 SANDWICHES

Pickled herring with egg salad, radish & tarragon

Boil the eggs for 7–8 minutes until hard-boiled. Peel, and then chop them finely. Combine with the mayonnaise and season, to taste.

Spread the butter evenly over the slices of bread.

Top each slice of buttered bread with pieces of herring followed by the egg salad and radish. Garnish with the tarragon leaves.

4 EGGS

2 TABLESPOONS MAYONNAISE

2 TABLESPOONS SALTED BUTTER

4 SLICES OF HEAVY DANISH RYE BREAD (SEE PAGES 231–233)

200 G (7 OZ) PICKLED HERRING, CHOPPED

4 RADISHES, THINLY SLICED

25 G (1 OZ) TARRAGON, LEAVES PICKED

Smoked pork, peas, pickled kohlrabi, yoghurt mustard crème & toasted buckwheat

Spread the butter evenly over the slices of bread.

Mix together the yoghurt and sweet mustard in a small bowl.

Top the buttered bread with the shredded pork, then spoon over the yoghurt dressing, the peas and kohlrabi. Finish by sprinkling with the buckwheat.

2 TABLESPOONS SALTED BUTTER

4 SLICES OF HEAVY DANISH RYE BREAD (SEE PAGES 231–33)

100 G (3½ OZ) NATURAL YOGHURT

1 TABLESPOON FINNISH SWEET MUSTARD (SEE PAGE 43), OR AMERICAN MUSTARD MIXED WITH 1 TEASPOON HONEY

150 G (5½ OZ) SALTED SMOKED PORK, SHREDDED

25 G (1 OZ) PEAS, THAWED IF FROZEN; IF USING FRESH PEAS BLANCH IN BOILING WATER FOR 2 MINUTES

50 G (1¾ OZ) KOHLRABI, LIGHTLY PICKLED (SEE PAGE 34)

2 TABLESPOONS TOASTED WHOLEGRAIN BUCKWHEAT (SEE PAGE 137)

Watercress crème, smoked salmon, pickled cucumber, dill and chips

Spread the butter evenly over the slices of bread. Mix the watercress and sour cream together in a small bowl.

Arrange the smoked salmon on the buttered bread and spoon over the watercress crème. Top with some pickled cucumber slices and garnish with sprigs of dill. Finally, use your hands to crush over some potato chips for an extra salty crunch.

2 TABLESPOONS SALTED BUTTER

4 SLICES OF HEAVY DANISH RYE BREAD (SEE PAGES 231–33)

A FEW SPRIGS OF WATERCRESS, LEAVES PICKED AND FINELY CHOPPED

100 G (3½ OZ) SOUR CREAM

150 G (5½ OZ) THINLY SLICED SMOKED SALMON

50 G (1¾ OZ) LIGHTLY PICKLED CUCUMBER SLICES (SEE PAGE 34)

25 G (1 OZ) DILL

HANDFUL OF SEA SALT POTATO CHIPS (CRISPS)

Rare beef, fried shallot, chunky remoulade, dill pickle & grated horseradish

Spread the butter evenly over the slices of bread. Top with the slices of beef, then spoon over the remoulade. Finish with the pickles and shallot, and grate over the fresh horseradish.

2 TABLESPOONS SALTED BUTTER

4 SLICES OF HEAVY DANISH RYE BREAD (SEE PAGES 231–33)

150 G (5½ OZ) RARE ROAST BEEF, SLICED

4 TABLESPOONS REMOULADE (SEE PAGE 97)

2 LARGE DILL PICKLES, THINLY SLICED

20 G (¾ OZ) FRIED SHALLOT

20 G (¾ OZ) FRESH HORSERADISH, PEELED (OR FROM A JAR)

Smoked chicken, apple, pickled carrots, hazelnut & raw broccoli

2 TABLESPOONS SALTED BUTTER

4 SLICES OF HEAVY DANISH RYE BREAD (SEE PAGES 231–33)

150 G (5½ OZ) SMOKED CHICKEN BREAST, SLICED

1 GRANNY SMITH APPLE, PEELED, CORED AND THINLY SLICED INTO ACIDULATED WATER

1 CARROT, THINLY SLICED AND LIGHTLY PICKLED (SEE PAGE 34)

25 G (1 OZ) TOASTED HAZELNUTS, CHOPPED

1 RAW BROCCOLI FLORET

Spread the butter evenly over the slices of bread. Top with the slices of chicken, apple and carrot and the hazelnuts. Use a mandoline to shave over the raw broccoli.

Smoked cheese, remoulade, celery, pickled red onion & *ymerdrys*

2 TABLESPOONS SALTED BUTTER

4 SLICES OF HEAVY DANISH RYE BREAD (SEE PAGES 231–33)

4 THICK SLICES OF SMOKED CHEESE

1 LARGE CELERY STALK, THINLY SLICED ON AN ANGLE

3 TABLESPOONS REMOULADE (SEE PAGE 97)

½ RED ONION, PEELED, THINLY SLICED AND LIGHTLY PICKLED (SEE PAGE 34)

20 G (¾ OZ) YMERDRYS OR CRUMBLED RYE CROUTONS (SEE PAGE 154)

Spread the butter evenly over the slices of bread. Top with the cheese slices, celery, remoulade and red onion. Sprinkle over the ymerdrys or rye croutons.

Skagenröra, cos & dill

In the Swedish culinary world, the word röra *means mix. Most commonly it refers to a creamy fish mixture used for topping open sandwiches (see pages 71–5).* Skagenröra, *using small prawns (shrimp), is the most popular version, paying homage to the seaside region of Skagen in north-west Denmark where seafood is abundant and brought to shore daily, but the concept can be applied to any seafood. The other famous combination is* gubbröra, *which is made from diced pickled herring, red onion, chives and crème fraîche. This is then spooned on top of half a hard-boiled egg, served on an open sandwich or with crispbreads. (A similar recipe can be found on page 125.)*

The only real rule is that dill and something creamy is used to bind the ingredients. In new Nordic cooking, crème fraîche or sour cream is most commonly used to provide creaminess, but it is sometimes mixed with mayonnaise. Experiment with your own combinations of ingredients: smoked fish with sour cream and lemon juice works a treat. This recipe is for the traditional skagenröra, *but served in the new-Nordic style, using lettuce leaf 'cups' instead of bread.*

SERVES 4

200 G (7 OZ) SMALL COOKED PRAWNS (SHRIMP), DRAINED, OR DEFROSTED IF FROZEN

2 TABLESPOONS CHOPPED DILL, PLUS EXTRA TO GARNISH

150 G (5½ OZ) CRÈME FRAÎCHE OR SOUR CREAM

1 TEASPOON FINNISH SWEET MUSTARD (SEE PAGE 43)

40 G (1½ OZ) CAVIAR OR FISH ROE (NO NEED FOR BELUGA!)

1 HEAD OF COS (ROMAINE) OR ICEBERG LETTUCE

SEEDY CRISPBREADS (SEE PAGE 227), TO SERVE

Combine the prawns, dill, crème fraîche or sour cream, mustard and the fish roe in a bowl to make the *rora*.

Wash and drain some lettuce leaves and arrange them on a platter. Spoon the *rora* into the lettuce 'cups'. Garnish with more dill and serve with crispbreads.

Potato waffles & gravlax

While Belgium may hold the European claim to waffles, there is no doubting their place in Nordic cuisine, especially when you consider the age of some of the cast-iron waffle makers around. The waffle dough in this recipe uses potatoes, providing a hearty savoury twist on the classic waffle that is usually served sweet. If you don't have a waffle maker, you could cook these like pancakes in a frying pan.

MAKES 4 THICK WAFFLES
DEPENDING ON THE SIZE OF YOUR WAFFLE MAKER

250 G (9 OZ) GRAVLAX OR SMOKED SALMON (SEE PAGE 37), THINLY SLICED

200 G (7 OZ) SOUR CREAM

½ RED ONION, THINLY SLICED, CURED FOR 10 MINUTES IN 1 TEASPOON CASTER (SUPERFINE) SUGAR AND THE JUICE OF ½ LEMON

1 LEMON, CUT INTO WEDGES

WAFFLES

250 G (9 OZ) POTATOES, PEELED

25 G (1 OZ) SALTED BUTTER, MELTED

60 G (2 OZ) PLAIN (ALL-PURPOSE) FLOUR

2 EGGS

PINCH OF WHITE PEPPER

1 TABLESPOON CHOPPED DILL, PLUS A FEW SPRIGS TO GARNISH

½ TEASPOON SALT

To make the waffles, boil the potatoes in a large saucepan of salted water for 12–15 minutes, until soft. Drain well, and allow to cool and dry out. For best results, put the potatoes through a ricer; alternatively, use a masher. Season to taste, then set aside and allow to cool.

In a large mixing bowl, combine the mashed potatoes with the melted butter, flour, eggs, white pepper, chopped dill and salt. Combine to form a wet dough similar to a thick pancake batter. Preheat the waffle maker.

Depending on the size of your waffle maker, spoon in an appropriate amount of mixture and cook for about 1 minute on each side, until golden brown at the edges.

Serve the waffles topped with gravlax, sour cream and red onion, with the lemon wedges to squeeze over, and some dill sprigs, to garnish.

Finnish pasties with egg butter

I ate these just near the border of Russia in the province of Karelia, which runs along the eastern side of Finland. I was on a tiny, 200 square metre (220 square yard) island for three days, experiencing Finnish midsummer – which seems to mainly involve a lot of aquavit! These Karelian treats could never be as nourishing as they were on that occasion, served for breakfast, warm out of the pan with lots of melting salty butter; nevertheless, cooked at home, they are perfect all year round when in need of some hearty, reviving carbs.

MAKES 15–20

100 ML (3½ FL OZ) FULL-CREAM (WHOLE) MILK

1 TABLESPOON SALTED BUTTER, MELTED, PLUS EXTRA TO SERVE

EGG BUTTER

4 EGGS

80 G (2¾ OZ) SALTED BUTTER, AT ROOM TEMPERATURE

1 TABLESPOON CHOPPED DILL

FILLING

1 TABLESPOON SALTED BUTTER

120 G (4½ OZ) SHORT-GRAIN RICE

650 ML (22 FL OZ) FULL-CREAM (WHOLE) MILK

DOUGH

300 G (10½ OZ) LIGHT RYE FLOUR, PLUS EXTRA FOR DUSTING

First make the filling. Bring 300 ml (10 fl oz) water and the butter to the boil in a saucepan and stir in the rice. Simmer for 10 minutes, stirring occasionally. Add the milk, increase the heat and stir until it boils. Reduce the heat to low and simmer with the lid on for about 50 minutes, or until the rice is just tender. Season with a pinch of salt then set aside to cool.

While the rice is cooling, boil the eggs for 7–8 minutes until hard-boiled. Peel, and then chop them finely. Combine with the room-temperature butter and the dill.

Make the dough by mixing together the flour, 150–200 ml (5–7 fl oz) water and a pinch of salt. Use your hands to knead the mixture until it forms a thick dough. Turn the dough out on to a lightly floured work surface and roll out to a thickness of about 2 mm (1/16 in); you can use a pasta-making machine for this.

Using an 8 cm (3¼ in) round cutter, cut out circles of dough; you should be able to get 15–20. Roll the circles a little thinner if possible, using some flour to help with the rolling.

Preheat the oven to its hottest temperature (around 275°C/525°F).

Spread a thin layer of the rice mixture into the middle of each dough circle. Bring up the sides of the pastry over the filling and crimp the dough. Place on a baking tray and cook for 15–20 minutes. Make sure the pasties don't burn, but you do want them to get so hot that the filling bubbles and blisters a little.

Mix the milk with the melted butter and brush over the top of the pasties. Place them on a tray and cover with a sheet of baking paper and a tea towel (dish towel). This will help them to soften.

Eat while still warm with the prepared egg and butter mixture spread over the top.

Pyttipanna

This Swedish 'scrape together' of ingredients shares the same heritage as bubble and squeak or steak hash: the idea being that you bring together left-over meat and vegetables in a pan for a hearty meal the day following a large roast dinner. Points of difference in the Swedish version include the mandatory inclusion of a pan-fried egg and some pickled beetroot (beets) on serving.

SERVES 4

50 G (1¾ OZ) SALTED BUTTER

300 G (10½ OZ) ROAST BEEF, CHOPPED INTO 1 CM (½ IN) DICE

100 G (3½ OZ) SPECK, OR PORK SAUSAGE, CHOPPED INTO 2 CM (¾ IN) DICE

SPLASH OF RAPESEED OIL

2 SMALL ONIONS, PEELED AND CHOPPED INTO 1 CM (½ IN) DICE

500 G (1 LB 2 OZ) BOILED POTATOES, CHOPPED INTO 2 CM (¾ IN) DICE

2 TABLESPOONS CHOPPED FLAT-LEAF PARSLEY

TO SERVE

4 EGGS

OIL OR SALTED BUTTER, FOR FRYING

250 G (9 OZ) PICKLED BEETROOT (BEETS) **(SEE PAGE 34)**

In a cast-iron pot or heavy-based frying pan melt half the butter over a medium heat.

Fry the beef and pork until they are warmed through and have taken on a little colour at the edges. Season, then transfer to a plate and set aside.

Add a splash of rapeseed oil and the remaining butter to the pan, and fry the onion for 4 minutes. Add the potato, cook for 2 minutes, then stir in the meat mixture until cooked through. Stir through the parsley.

In a separate non-stick frying pan, fry the eggs sunny side up in oil or butter. Serve the *pyttipanna* topped with an egg and some pickled beetroot.

Hasselback potatoes & Jansson's temptation

These dishes were big in the eighties and all baby boomers will remember eating them off a white linen tablecloth at some point. The hasselback is genius: multiple cuts into the potato allow the fat to crisp up the edges and cook the potato through more quickly. I'm surprised we don't see them more often. Jansson himself is of somewhat ambiguous origin, with no one quite certain who he was, but his temptation is certainly utterly, dangerously irresistible! For any lover of salty fish flavours, its marriage with cream and potatoes plus a crunchy breadcrumb topping is just too much. You may pay the price later though because you don't get a sense of quite how much cream you are consuming when you eat it. They both go well with meat and fish dishes.

BOTH SERVE 4 AS A SIDE DISH

Hasselback potatoes

16 SMALL NEW POTATOES

125 G (4½ OZ) UNSALTED BUTTER, MELTED

SEA SALT

Preheat the oven to 200°C (400°F). Peel the potatoes, then use the peeler to shape each one into a smooth, rounded egg shape. Without cutting all the way through, thinly slice the potatoes crossways all the way along their length. Place them on a baking tray and gently press down on each potato to fan the slices in one direction. Brush them all over with as much of the melted butter as is needed to cover them, and season with salt.

Roast the potatoes for 25–30 minutes, brushing them occasionally with the remaining butter. They should be soft enough in the middle that a fork passes through easily, while the tops are golden brown and crisp.

Jansson's temptation

1 MEDIUM TO LARGE ONION, THINLY SLICED

50 G (1¾ OZ) SALTED BUTTER, PLUS EXTRA FOR FRYING AND GREASING

600 G (1 LB 5 OZ) POTATOES, PEELED

125 G (4½ OZ) TINNED SPRATS OR HERRING IN SWEET BRINE (50 G OR 1.75 OZ OF ITALIAN ANCHOVIES WITH 1 TABLESPOON OF SUGAR CAN BE USED AS A SUBSTITUTE)

200–250 ML (7–8½ FL OZ) POURING (SINGLE/LIGHT) CREAM

PINCH OF WHITE PEPPER

35 G (1¼ OZ/⅓ CUP) DRY BREADCRUMBS

Sauté the onion in 1 tablespoon butter for 4–6 minutes, or until soft and golden. Do not let it brown. Remove from the heat and set aside.

Cut the potatoes into matchsticks. This is easily done using a food processor fitted with a julienne disc, a mandoline or another slicing device. Make sure you have at least 500 g (1 lb 2 oz) potato matchsticks. If you like, you can plunge the potato briefly into cold water to remove some of the starch. This will prevent the potato from sticking together too much while the dish is cooking. Drain thoroughly.

Preheat the oven to 200°C (400°F). Reserving the brine, drain the sprat fillets.

Grease a shallow, 2–3 litre (68–101 fl oz/8–12 cups) gratin dish with butter. Spread about one-third of the potato matchsticks across the base then top with half the sprats and half the onions. Repeat the layers, finishing with a layer of potato.

Mix half the cream with 2 tablespoons of the reserved brine and the white pepper. Pour the mixture over the ingredients in the gratin dish then dot the surface with half of the butter. Bake for 30 minutes, then remove from the oven and pour the rest of the cream over the top. If the gratin still seems very moist, you may not need to use all of the cream; on the other hand, you may need to use extra if it has started to dry out. Scatter over the breadcrumbs and dot with the remaining butter. Bake for a further 15–30 minutes, until the gratin has a creamy soft consistency and the top is nicely browned. The timing will depend mostly on the size and depth of your baking dish – keep an eye on it during baking to ensure it doesn't dry out.

Herring, potato & lingonberry

I love nothing more than a crunchy coating around a piece of fish paired with a hit of something sour, usually just a simple squeeze of lemon. This recipe uses a very quick and easy method for coating fish, dispensing with the messier, traditional French way involving dipping the fillets into egg and then flour. Instead of lemon, the required tartness is provided by lingonberry jam. Small mackerel fillets or sardines make good substitutes for herring; both are a little saltier but will do the trick nicely.

SERVES 4

50 G (1¾ OZ/½ CUP) WHITE FLOUR

35 G (1¼ OZ/⅓ CUP) DRY BREADCRUMBS

2 TABLESPOONS CHOPPED DILL, PLUS EXTRA TO GARNISH

800 G (1 LB 12 OZ) HERRING FILLETS, DORSAL FINS REMOVED

50 G (1¾ OZ) SALTED BUTTER

50 ML (1¾ FL OZ) SUNFLOWER OIL

LINGONBERRY JAM, TO SERVE

MASHED POTATOES

800 G (1 LB 12 OZ) POTATOES, PEELED

100 ML (3½ FL OZ) FULL-CREAM (WHOLE) MILK

100 ML (3½ FL OZ) POURING (SINGLE/LIGHT) CREAM

25 G (1 OZ) SALTED BUTTER

For the mashed potatoes, boil the potatoes in a large saucepan of salted water for 12–15 minutes, until soft. Drain well, and allow to cool and dry out. (Returning them to the hot pan can help with this.)

Gently heat the milk, cream and butter in a large saucepan until just warm and until the butter has melted. For best results, put the potatoes through a ricer; alternatively, use a masher. Mix the potatoes into the creamy, buttery mixture using a wooden spoon. Season to taste, then set aside and keep warm.

Mix together the flour, breadcrumbs, a little salt and the dill in a shallow dish. Coat the fish thoroughly in this mixture and use a little of the mix to sandwich 2 fillets together, skin sides facing out. Repeat with all the fish.

Melt the butter with the sunflower oil in a non-stick or cast-iron frying pan over a medium heat. Fry the paired fillets for 3 minutes, flipping them over halfway through so they cook evenly.

Serve with the mashed potatoes, lingonberry jam and garnish with some extra dill.

If you are feeling indulgent freshly made brown butter (see page 46) provides a luxurious extra layer when poured straight from the pan over the fish and mash.

Meatballs

What makes Nordic meatballs different from Italian ones? Well, for a start they are not swimming in a rich tomato ragu; it is the cream-soaked breadcrumbs and hint of allspice that I think really sets them apart. I also recommend using a blender to make the mince as fine as you can. Make double, as they freeze well.

SERVES 4 VERY GENEROUSLY OR WITH LEFTOVERS

LINGONBERRY JAM, TO SERVE

LIGHTLY PICKLED CUCUMBER (SEE PAGE 34), TO SERVE

MASHED POTATOES

800 G (1 LB 12 OZ) POTATOES, PEELED

100 ML (3½ FL OZ) FULL-CREAM (WHOLE) MILK

100 ML (3½ FL OZ) POURING (SINGLE/LIGHT) CREAM

25 G (1 OZ) SALTED BUTTER

MEATBALLS

50 G (1¾ OZ/½ CUP) DRY BREADCRUMBS

2 PINCHES OF GROUND ALLSPICE

2 TEASPOONS SALT

½ TEASPOON WHITE PEPPER

200 ML (7 FL OZ) FULL-CREAM (WHOLE) MILK

2 SMALL ONIONS, PEELED

500 G (1 LB 2 OZ) MINCED (GROUND) BEEF

500 G (1 LB 2 OZ) MINCED (GROUND) PORK

2 EGGS, WHISKED

1–2 TABLESPOONS RAPESEED OIL

1–2 TABLESPOONS SALTED BUTTER

BROWN SAUCE

600 ML (20½ FL OZ) BEEF STOCK (PREFERABLY HOMEMADE)

2 TABLESPOONS PLAIN (ALL-PURPOSE) FLOUR

2–3 TABLESPOONS SALTED BUTTER

100 ML (3½ FL OZ) POURING (SINGLE/LIGHT) CREAM

1 TABLESPOON ORANGE JUICE

For the mashed potatoes, boil the potatoes in a large saucepan of salted water for 12–15 minutes, until soft. Drain well, and allow to cool and dry out.

Heat the milk, cream and butter for the potatoes in a large saucepan. For best results, put the potatoes through a ricer, or use a masher. Mix them into the buttery mixture using a wooden spoon. Season to taste, then set aside.

For the meatballs, combine the breadcrumbs, allspice, salt and white pepper in a large bowl. Mix in the milk to form a smooth paste then let stand for 10 minutes. If the mixture is still quite dry, add a little more milk.

Grate the onion extremely finely or purée it in a blender.

Line a baking tray with baking paper. Use your hands to knead together the minced meats, onion, eggs and the breadcrumb paste until well combined, or mix together in a food processor. With clean, wet hands form the mixture into meatballs, about 2.5–3 cm (1–1¼ in) wide. Place on the lined baking tray.

For the sauce, bring the stock to a boil. Sprinkle the flour into a dry saucepan over a medium heat. Using a wooden spatula, stir the flour for a few minutes, until it turns golden brown. Be careful not to burn it, or you will have to start again. Quickly stir in the butter until the flour is fully incorporated; you may need extra butter. Immediately pour in the hot stock, a little at a time, stirring to ensure the mixture is smooth. Strain through a sieve if there are any lumps. Wipe the pan clean, return the gravy, add the cream and continue cooking over a medium heat, stirring occasionally, until it thickens. Add a little more stock (or water) if it is too thick. Stir in the orange juice, check the seasoning and set aside.

Preheat the oven to 140°C (275°F). Heat the oil and butter in a cast-iron or heavy-based pan over a medium heat until the butter foams. In batches, cook the meatballs for 10 minutes, until browned on all sides. Keep them warm in the oven while you cook the rest, using more oil and butter as necessary.

Reheat the gravy, whisking to smooth it out. Gently reheat the mash. Serve the meatballs and mash 'swimming' in gravy with a dollop of lingonberry jam and some lightly pickled cucumber.

Fisk frikadeller

To the outside world, the Swedes have crowned themselves the meatball kings, but in Nordic countries, the famous Danish fish version carries a lot of sway. Tradition sees them served with a Nordic take on the French classic remoulade. Essentially, it is a twist on tartare sauce with a yellow tint coming from either turmeric or curry powder. And, like all fish and mayonnaise pairings, it works brilliantly.

The key to making excellent frikadeller *is to ensure the 'batter' is as light as possible. If you add too much liquid and the mixture is not kept cold the patties are very hard to handle and will fall apart in the pan. Add as much milk as the mix requires but make sure they are kept cold before frying. I have served these fluffy fishcakes with boiled broccoli and thin slices of raw broccoli stem, lightly pickled (see page 34).*

SERVES 4

300 G (10½ OZ) BROCCOLI, TO SERVE

LIGHTLY PICKLED BROCCOLI STEM (SEE PAGE 34), TO SERVE

FRIKADELLER

500 G (1 LB 2 OZ) COD OR DORY FILLETS

1 SMALL ONION, PEELED AND QUARTERED

1 TEASPOON SALT

75 G (2½ OZ/½ CUP) PLAIN (ALL-PURPOSE) FLOUR

1 EGG

PINCH OF WHITE PEPPER

½ TEASPOON BAKING POWDER

100 ML (3½ FL OZ) FULL-CREAM (WHOLE) MILK, OR MORE IF YOUR MIXTURE ALLOWS IT

SALTED BUTTER AND OIL, FOR FRYING

REMOULADE

60 G (2 OZ/¼ CUP) MAYONNAISE

60 G (2 OZ/¼ CUP) GREEK-STYLE YOGHURT

1 TABLESPOON CHOPPED FLAT-LEAF PARSLEY AND/OR DILL

2 TABLESPOONS FINELY CHOPPED RED ONION

2 TABLESPOONS FINELY CHOPPED DILL PICKLES

2 TEASPOONS FRESH LEMON JUICE

1 TEASPOON MILD CURRY POWDER, WHITE PEPPER OR TURMERIC, TO TASTE

In a food processor blend the fish and onion to a fine purée. Add the salt, flour, egg, white pepper, baking powder and as much milk as the mixture allows – it should resemble a cake batter. Transfer to a bowl and chill in the refrigerator for 20 minutes.

Meanwhile, make the remoulade by mixing all the ingredients together. Chill.

Melt the butter and oil in a non-stick frying pan over a medium heat. Using two large cold spoons, shape the chilled fish mixture into patties and place them straight in the pan. The cold spoons will help the patties keep their shape. Fry for 4–5 minutes on each side, until cooked through.

Meanwhile, boil or steam the broccoli for 8–10 minutes, until just tender.

Serve the hot patties with chopped broccoli, the remoulade and thin slices of lightly pickled broccoli stem.

Meatloaf, cucumber & brown sauce

I don't know why rissoles and meatloaf get such a bad rap; they are so good! They have a tender, light texture that is a delight to my palate, and they are more easily digested than whole meats. Veal mince is commonly used in traditional Nordic home-cooked meals, and it makes for an even lighter meatloaf, especially when mixed with breadcrumbs and milk. This recipe also uses the classic gravy-like 'brun sauce', typical in traditional Nordic cooking.

SERVES 4

500 G (1 LB 2 OZ) NEW POTATOES, UNPEELED

25 G (1 OZ) SALTED BUTTER

1 X QUANTITY BROWN SAUCE (SEE PAGE 94)

1 CARROT, THINLY SLICED AND LIGHTLY PICKLED (SEE PAGE 34)

MEATLOAF

35 G (1¼ OZ/⅓ CUP) DRY BREADCRUMBS

100 ML (3½ FL OZ) FULL-CREAM (WHOLE) MILK

1 TEASPOON SALT

PINCH OF WHITE PEPPER

1 TABLESPOON DIJON MUSTARD

½ ONION, PEELED AND GRATED

3 SLICES OF PROSCIUTTO OR SMOKED BACON, CHOPPED (IF USING BACON, FRY IT IN A LITTLE OIL UNTIL JUST COOKED)

1 TABLESPOON THICK (DOUBLE/HEAVY) CREAM

700 G (1 LB 9 OZ) MINCED (GROUND) VEAL

1 TABLESPOON RAPESEED OIL, FOR FRYING

1 TABLESPOON SALTED BUTTER, FOR FRYING

LIGHTLY PICKLED CHARRED CUCUMBER

1 LARGE CUCUMBER

1 TEASPOON CIDER VINEGAR

Preheat the oven to 180°C (350°F). Line a 25 cm x 10 cm (10 in x 4 in) loaf (bar) tin with baking paper. Soak the breadcrumbs in the milk in a blender for 3 minutes. Purée with the remaining meatloaf ingredients except the oil and butter.

Scrape the mixture into the prepared loaf tin, then place in a deep roasting tray. Transfer to the oven and pour cold water into the roasting tray so that it comes at least halfway up the sides of the loaf tin. Cook for 30–40 minutes, or until a probe thermometer inserted into the middle reaches 70°C (160°F). If you don't have a thermometer, slice into the loaf and make sure it's cooked through. Remove the meatloaf from the oven and let it cool in its tin for at least 20 minutes. When cool enough to handle, remove from the tin and slice into 12 cm x 3 cm x 3 cm (4¾ in x 1¼ in x 1¼ in) batons.

While the meatloaf is cooling, boil the potatoes in a large saucepan of salted water for 10 minutes, until a knife passes through them easily. Drain well, and allow to cool and dry out. (Returning them to the hot pan can help with this.)

Preheat the grill (broiler) or a chargrill pan until hot. Halve the cucumber and scrape out and discard the seeds. Cut into batons a similar size to the meatloaf slices. Cook the cucumber briefly, just until they take on some char marks; do not cook them for so long that they collapse. Transfer them to a bowl and chill in the refrigerator. When cold, toss with the vinegar and a pinch of salt. Set aside.

Press down on the potatoes using the palm of your hand until they crack slightly. Melt the butter in a non-stick frying pan over a medium heat and fry the potatoes for a couple of minutes on each side until their skins take on some colour. Transfer to a bowl and keep warm.

Fry the meatloaf batons in the same pan, in the butter and oil. Turn them over once so that at least two sides caramelise slightly and develop a crisp edge.

Reheat the brown sauce and aerate it using a coffee frother or whisk, if you like. Divide the potatoes, meatloaf batons and cucumber between serving plates and pour over the sauce. Top with the lightly pickled carrot.

Kalops stew

This traditional stew is believed to have been developed during the 1800s, when Sweden was heavily influenced by British cuisine. The name comes from the old English word 'collops', referring to 'pieces of meat'. Hailing from Skane in south Sweden, its distinct aromatic flavour is due to the combination of white pepper and allspice, a popular import in the region. Allspice is not a mix of spices, as most people think; it is actually a very aromatic berry with flavour notes similar to cloves, cinnamon and nutmeg. Traditionally served with pickled beetroot (beets) – yes, another one! – here, I have topped the stew with some meltingly soft leeks, pickled parsnip and chopped toasted hazelnuts for a texture contrast.

SERVES 4–6

1 TABLESPOON RAPESEED OIL

2 TABLESPOONS SALTED BUTTER

1 KG (2 LB 3 OZ) STEWING BEEF PIECES, SUCH AS CHUCK

½ TEASPOON WHITE PEPPER

1 TABLESPOON PLAIN (ALL-PURPOSE) FLOUR

1 TABLESPOON RED WINE VINEGAR

2 TOMATOES, CHOPPED

2 ONIONS, CHOPPED

4 CARROTS, ROUGHLY CHOPPED INTO 2 CM (¾ IN) PIECES

2 TEASPOONS CASTER (SUPERFINE) SUGAR

8 DRIED ALLSPICE BERRIES

3 BAY LEAVES

1 PARSNIP

HEAVY PICKLING SOLUTION (SEE PAGE 34)

600 G (1 LB 5 OZ) POTATOES, PEELED

25 G (1 OZ) TOASTED HAZELNUTS, CHOPPED, TO GARNISH

LEEK

2 TABLESPOONS SALTED BUTTER

½ LEEK, GREEN PART (MIDDLE-THIRD) ONLY, HALVED LENGTHWAYS

Heat half the rapeseed oil and half the butter in a large heavy-based saucepan. Season the beef with salt and white pepper and brown for about 4 minutes in the hot fat. When coloured all over, sprinkle with the flour and cook, stirring the meat around until the pan becomes dry.

Add the vinegar and 2 tablespoons water and use these to deglaze the pan, scraping up any bits stuck to the bottom. Transfer to a flameproof casserole dish and add the tomatoes.

Clean the original pan and sauté the onions and carrots in the remaining oil and butter until the onions are soft and translucent. Tip into the casserole with the sugar, allspice and bay leaves. Pour in enough water to just cover the meat.

Bring to the boil, then reduce to a simmer and cook with the lid on for about 1 hour.

Stir the stew occasionally and halfway through cooking check the liquid level to see it has not dried out; top up if needed.

Slice the parsnip into thin rounds, put in a non-metallic bowl, pour over the pickling solution and leave to pickle for at least 20 minutes.

After the stew has been cooking for 35 minutes, get the potatoes on to boil and while they are cooking prepare the leek. Preheat the oven to 180°C (350°F). Rub the butter on a sheet of foil and place the leek, cut side down, on top. Wrap in the foil, place on a baking tray and cook in the oven for 15 minutes until deliciously soft.

Serve the stew with the boiled potatoes and the leeks, garnished with the chopped hazelnuts and drained parsnip slices.

HOTEL
BROSUNDET
T.BERSET AS

Cinnamon buns

I called these cinnamon buns to get your attention! They do contain cinnamon but they also have cardamom in them, and I think they are all the better for it. The Nordics have a long appreciation for cardamom spanning all the way back to the Vikings' first taste of this exotic spice during their attacks on Constantinople.

This is a very forgiving dough, so use it as your basic recipe and get creative with the fillings. Go for spices, pastes or thick jams; avoid very wet fillings. Some less traditional flavours I have tried include fig and fennel, and vanilla and saffron. In Iceland, they are topped with icing, like American doughnuts.

MAKES ABOUT 16 BUNS

100 G (3½ OZ) UNSALTED BUTTER, AT ROOM TEMPERATURE

300 ML (7 FL OZ) FULL-CREAM (WHOLE) MILK

18 G (¾ OZ) DRIED INSTANT YEAST

110 G (5 OZ) CASTER (SUPERFINE) SUGAR

700 G (1 LB 9 OZ) PLAIN (ALL-PURPOSE) FLOUR

1 LARGE EGG

PINCH OF SALT

1 TEASPOON GROUND CARDAMOM

FILLING

120 G BUTTER

60 G SUGAR

1.5 TABLESPOONS GROUND CINNAMON

1 TABLESPOON CARDAMOM SEEDS (OUT OF POD) GROUND WITH MORTAR & PESTLE

GLAZING SYRUP

1 EGG, BEATEN

50 ML (1¾ FL OZ) GOLDEN SYRUP OR TREACLE MIXED WITH 1 TABLESPOON WATER

2 TABLESPOONS CASTER (SUPERFINE) SUGAR

To make the dough, melt the butter in the microwave or in a saucepan over low heat. Combine the milk and dry yeast in a mixer with a dough hook or a large bowl. Add the butter to the milk and start the mixer on low speed, adding in the remaining dough ingredients.

After a minute or so, check if it needs a splash more milk or more flour. It should have come together and should be moving in the mixer as a mass. If the mixer is struggling add a splash of milk. Continue to knead in mixer for 10 minutes or if by hand for 15 minutes.

The resulting dough should be smooth, elastic and with a slight stickiness. Let it rest for 1 hour in a warm place covered with a wet clean tea towel. If your kitchen is cool like mine - place it in a very low oven, no more than 50°C (120°F).

Flatten the dough and roll it into a 40 cm (12 in) x 25 cm (10 in) rectangle. Fold the shorter edges in to meet each other, then fold again. Spin it 90 degrees then roll out again to create a 40 cm (12 in) x 25cm (10 in) rectangle. Use a ruler to measure 2.5 cm (1 in) strips , cutting vertically with the shortest edge.

Pick up each strip, slightly stretch it at both ends and roll it around three fingers. When 10 cm (4 in) is left, anchor the dough with your thumb and pull that 10 cm (4 in) over the top of the spiral before tucking it underneath to replace the space occupied by your three fingers. Continue with all the buns and place on two baking trays lined with baking paper. Cover them with clean tea towels and rest for 2 hours.

Preheat the oven to 210°C (410°F).

Mix an egg with 2 tablespoons of water and brush the buns with the egg wash. Bake for 10 minutes, rotating the trays halfway through cooking.

As soon as they are out of the oven brush them with glazing syrup or molasses mixed with water. Sprinkle with sugar and allow to cool slightly before serving. They will keep for a few days and are best stored in paper bags or sealed containers.

Nordic granola

There is so much satisfaction to be had in making home-made granola. First of all the kitchen smells incredible for a couple of hours, secondly you save some coin because boutique granolas fetch ludicrous prices, and most importantly you get to be creative with what goes in the mix.

Quite often in our kitchen the pantry will dictate what's going in, but this is my ideal combination.

MAKES ABOUT 14 SERVINGS

Preheat the oven to 130°C (265°F). Line two baking trays with baking paper.

Place all the ingredients, except for the coconut flakes, oats and dried berries, in a very large bowl and mix everything together well.

Stir the oats through the granola mixture, then spread it out over the prepared baking trays in an even layer. Bake in the preheated oven for 1 hour moving the mixture around every 20 minutes for even cooking, adding the coconut flakes for the last 10 minutes of cooking, until golden. (To ensure even cooking you may have to rotate the trays during this time.)

Turn off the oven and leave the granola to cool in it with the door left slightly ajar. Once cool, remove the granola trays from the oven and sprinkle over the dried berries, then transfer to suitable airtight containers or jars. Serve the granola with yoghurt, milk or oat milk and fresh fruit, or with fruit nectar and yoghurt.

100 G (3½ OZ/1 CUP) SPELT FLAKES

125 G (4½ OZ/1 CUP) BUCKWHEAT FLAKES

100 G (3½ OZ/1 CUP) RYE FLAKES

90 G (3¼ OZ/ ½2 CUP) PEPITAS (PUMPKIN SEEDS)

60 G (2¼ OZ/ ½ CUP) SUNFLOWER KERNELS

140 G (5 OZ/1 CUP) HAZELNUTS, CHOPPED

100 ML (3½ FL OZ) LINGONBERRY CORDIAL (SYRUP)

4 TABLESPOONS RAPESEED OIL

2 TEASPOONS CARDAMOM SEEDS, CRUSHED (OPEN THE PODS TO REMOVE THE SEEDS INSIDE)

1 TEASPOON GROUND CINNAMON

2 TABLESPOONS SESAME SEEDS

PINCH OF SALT

55 G (2 OZ/1 CUP) COCONUT FLAKES

240 G (9 OZ/3 CUPS) ROLLED (PORRIDGE) OATS

100 G (3½ OZ) DRIED BERRIES (I LIKE BLUEBERRIES AND LINGONBERRIES, BUT YOU COULD USE CRANBERRIES, RAISINS, ETC.)

CHAPTER FOUR

From the Sea

NECESSE EST VIVERE NON EST NECESSE
Nautisk
BIBLIOTEKSKARTA
FYRMASTAD BARK

Nordic countries are surrounded by sea and at almost every turn inland you will find a lake or a river. The varying salt levels and temperatures found across the region result in a rich abundance of fish species to be celebrated in the kitchen. It is no wonder that fish and seafood form a central part of new Nordic cooking.

In days gone by, preserving methods, such as salting, drying, fermenting and smoking (see Chapter One) were necessary to provide for leaner times. During the winter, the harsh weather conditions made fishing an arduous endeavour. Even today, ice covers the waterways in the northern reaches for a good part of the year. Recently, however, fishing has become an increasingly popular pastime. I've even seen caravans set directly on the ice with a hole cut through the bottom straight into the water – from sea to caravan and into a pan, it doesn't get much fresher than that.

Today, Nordic chefs continue to preserve and cook fish in the traditional ways in order to obtain those wonderful unique flavours. And nowhere more so than in Sweden, where they appear to have more ways than any other country for preparing fish. With this multitude of cooking techniques comes a multitude of serving ideas, including attempts to match the fish with other local ingredients, such as cheeses, fruits and jams.

Mackerel, herring and salmon are all strong, oily fish, packing a lot of punch in the flavour department. This means they can stand up to almost any ingredient: herring with cheese, salmon with feta and bacon. Some work, while others take a bit of getting used to! In this chapter I explore some traditional preparation and serving ideas, as well as some newer techniques for enjoying these fruits of the water.

Oysters, apple cider granita & liquorice

Denmark's affinity with liquorice gets a proper mention in the Sweets chapter (see page 271), but its pairing with salt is likely to seem baffling until you've tried it. Here it combines with the true taste of the sea, the oyster, along with the delightfully refreshing sweetness of an apple cider and cucumber granita. It is an unusual and winning combination that is incredibly refreshing on a hot day.

SERVES 6

500 ML (17 FL OZ/2 CUPS) APPLE CIDER

1 TELEGRAPH CUCUMBER, PEELED, HALVED LENGTHWAYS AND SEEDS REMOVED

1 TABLESPOON LIQUORICE POWDER, TO TASTE

24 OYSTERS

ROCK SALT, TO SET THE OYSTERS ON

To make the granita, blend the cider and cucumber together. Transfer to a shallow 30 cm x 20 cm (12 in x 8 in) dish and freeze for at least 4 hours.

Half an hour before serving, let the granita sit at room temperature for 5 minutes, then, using a fork, pull through the top half of the ice to turn it into 'snow'. Return to the freezer for 10 minutes, then repeat.

Open the oysters, top with a spoonful of the granita and sprinkle over the liquorice powder, to taste. Serve on a bed of wet rock salt.

Mussels, brown butter, dill & apple

In this simple dish, the sweetness and nuttiness of brown butter complements the pure, salty flavour of mussels beautifully, while the apple-cider vinegar does a great job of replacing the traditional lemon juice. Try to hunt down the best quality vinegar you can find – the cloudy, uglier, unpasteurised variety being better than the crystal clear kind as it retains its nutrients.

SERVES 6

2 KG (4 LB 8 OZ) BLUE MUSSELS

150 G (5½ OZ) UNSALTED BUTTER

2 TABLESPOONS RAPESEED OIL

4 SHALLOTS, FINELY DICED

3 TABLESPOONS APPLE-CIDER VINEGAR

1 TABLESPOON SEA SALT FLAKES

3 TABLESPOONS CHOPPED DILL

1 GRANNY SMITH APPLE, PEELED, CORED AND GRATED

Discard any broken mussels, or open ones that don't close when tapped on the bench. Scrub and pull out the hairy beards and rinse well. When cooked, discard any unopened mussels.

Melt the butter in a heavy-based saucepan and cook for 2–3 minutes, until it is foaming, turning brown and you can smell a nutty aroma. Remove the pan from the heat and transfer it to a cold surface to stop the cooking. The butter will continue to cook in the pan, so if you feel like it is getting too dark, pour it into another vessel. Set aside.

Heat the oil and shallots in a lidded pot over a low–medium heat until the shallots are translucent and slightly soft, about 4 minutes. Add the mussels, vinegar and sea salt, increase the heat to the high, cover with the lid and cook for 3 minutes. Give the pot a good shake to try and bring those mussels that are at the bottom of the pot to the top and cook for a further 3 minutes. Once almost all the mussels have opened, stir through the brown butter, dill and apple and cook for 30 seconds more. Serve immediately with a good lager and some dark rye bread.

Spinach soup, fish roe & egg

This is a fine example of new Nordic cooking mixing earthy flavours with tastes of the sea. It draws influence from a classic Swedish soup made with nettles and served with an egg on top. In this recipe, the texture and salty explosion from the roe provides a much-appreciated contrast to the smooth spinach and broccoli. Visually, it's a winner too.

SERVES 4

4 EGGS

120 G (4½ OZ) BROCCOLI, ROUGHLY BROKEN INTO FLORETS

200 G (7 OZ) FRESH SPINACH LEAVES

25 G (1 OZ) SALTED BUTTER

1 TABLESPOON NATURAL YOGHURT

250 ML (8½ FL OZ/1 CUP) WARM FISH STOCK OR JUST-BOILED WATER

75 G (2¾ OZ) FISH ROE OR CAVIAR

Boil the eggs for 7–8 minutes until hard-boiled. Cool under running water and leave in a bowl of cold water for at least 5 minutes.

Meanwhile, boil the broccoli in salted water for 4–5 minutes, until a knife passes easily through the stems. Drain.

Blend the broccoli, spinach, butter and yoghurt. Gradually add the warm stock or just-boiled water while still blending. Once combined, season to taste, then divide between serving bowls. Peel the eggs then grate them over the top and garnish with spoonfuls of the roe.

Smoked eel, leek & scrambled egg

Smoked eel has a great natural sweetness and if you combine it, as in this recipe, with buttery leeks and egg, you can't go wrong. I love this for breakfast with toasted bread. When seasoning the dish, keep in mind that the eel is already very salty.

SERVES 4

250 G (9 OZ) SMOKED EEL, SKIN AND BONE REMOVED, FLAKED

CRUSTY BREAD, TO SERVE

LEEK

60 G (2 OZ) SALTED BUTTER

1 SMALL LEEK, GREEN PART (MIDDLE-THIRD) ONLY, HALVED LENGTHWAYS AND CROSSWAYS

PINCH OF WHITE PEPPER

SCRAMBLED EGG

100 ML (3½ FL OZ) POURING (SINGLE/LIGHT) CREAM

8 EGGS

WHITE PEPPER

Preheat the oven to 180°C (350°F). Rub half the butter for the leek on a sheet of foil and lay the leek, cut side down, on top. Season with white pepper and wrap in the foil. Place on a baking tray and cook for 15 minutes.

Meanwhile, whisk the cream with the eggs in a large bowl. Season with salt and white pepper. Place the flaked eel on a plate next to the stove top.

When the leek is cooked, melt the remaining butter in a large non-stick frying pan over a medium heat. Add the leek, eel and eggs all at once. Scramble to your liking but remove from the heat before it is fully cooked as it will keep cooking in the pan. Transfer to plates and serve with crusty bread.

Flaked salmon burger, parsnip fries & horseradish

Salmon is often the first ingredient people think of when considering Nordic cooking. Unfortunately, wild salmon is not as prevalent as you would think. Because of this, I often find that, from supermarkets to fish stalls, it can taste pretty similar the world over because it is most commonly farmed, and it can have quite an overpowering flavour. Nordic salmon is, perhaps, a little more understated in terms of taste, but I usually prefer to use ocean trout. It is a very similar fish in terms of texture, but with a more subtle flavour. The fish burger recipe below gives a nod to the soft bun and soft meat culture coming over from America. You will need a kitchen thermometer for this recipe.

SERVES 4

700 ML (23½ FL OZ) SUNFLOWER OIL, OR ENOUGH TO SUBMERGE THE FISH IN THE POT

3 JUNIPER BERRIES

1 X 800 G (1 LB 12 OZ) FRESH SALMON OR OCEAN TROUT FILLET

800 G (1 LB 12 OZ) PARSNIPS

½ TELEGRAPH CUCUMBER

100 ML (3½ FL OZ) SWEET PICKLING SOLUTION (SEE PAGE 34)

FRESHLY GRATED NUTMEG, TO TASTE

4 TABLESPOONS REMOULADE (SEE PAGE 97)

4 SWEET SOFT BREAD BUNS

50 G (1¾ OZ) FRESH HORSERADISH, PEELED AND JULIENNED, KEPT IN A WATER BATH (ALTERNATIVELY, USE THE KIND YOU BUY IN A JAR)

To confit the salmon, gently heat the sunflower oil with the juniper berries in a large heavy-based saucepan until the oil reaches 55°C (131°F). Carefully slide the salmon into the pan – if the fillet is too large to fit comfortably, cut it in half crossways. The temperature should drop to 45°C (113°F). Cook, maintaining this temperature for 15–20 minutes, until it breaks apart when you pull at it with a fork. Keep testing the temperature of the oil. The aim is not to cook the salmon but to change its taste and texture through gentle heating. Remove the fish from the oil with slotted spoons and wrap it in foil. Set aside, near the stove top to keep warm. Increase the heat under the oil until it reaches 190–200°C (375–400°F).

While the fish is cooking, peel and cut the parsnips into batons about 10 cm (4 in) long and 1–2 cm (½–¾ in) wide.

Use a mandoline or peeler to slice the cucumber into ribbons. Pickle it in the sweet pickling solution for 20 minutes before serving. (Remove the cucumber with a fork so you can use the pickling solution again.)

When the oil is hot enough, fry the parsnips in two or three batches for 3–4 minutes, until golden brown. Keep the temperature of the oil high otherwise the fries will be soggy; don't overcrowd the pan. Transfer to paper towel to drain, then grate over a little nutmeg and season with salt.

To serve, spread some remoulade on to the base of each bun. Flake chunks of the fish over each one, and top with some pickled cucumber and a few strands of the fresh horseradish. Serve with the parsnip fries.

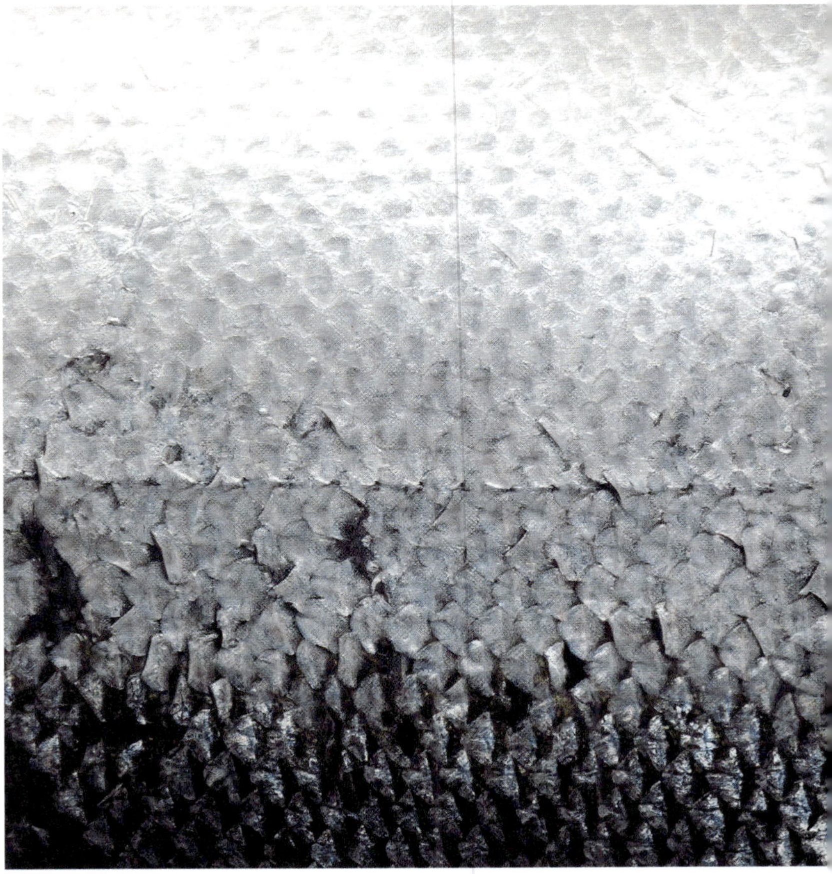

Sill, dill & omelette sandwich

From Odense to Reykjavik, no smorgasbord, Danish smørrebrød selection (see pages 72–5) or Christmas table can escape the pickled herring, also known as sill *or* sild. *The variety of preparation methods is endless, but I find that its strong, sweet and salty flavour always seems to dominate whatever dish it is in. That said, I love it. You can't go wrong combining it with new potatoes or sitting it on top of a crispbread with some crunchy cucumber slices. But I fully admit that for newcomers to this special fish, the flavours can be a bit overwhelming. So with a nod to the Nordics' neighbours to the east, this mayonnaise mix, similar to a Russian salad, softens the intensity of the herring. Pickled herring is readily available from that large Swedish furniture retailer or Eastern European delis.*

SERVES 4

1 TABLESPOON SALTED BUTTER

3 EGGS, BEATEN

250 G (9 OZ) PICKLED HERRING, DRAINED AND CUT INTO 2 CM (¾ IN) DICE

1 RED ONION, ½ FINELY DICED, ½ THINLY SLICED

1½ TABLESPOONS MAYONNAISE

1 TABLESPOON CHOPPED DILL

50 G (1¾ OZ) PEAS, THAWED IF FROZEN; IF USING FRESH PEAS BLANCH IN BOILING WATER FOR 2 MINUTES

1 BAGUETTE

250 G (9 OZ) ICEBERG LETTUCE, THINLY SLICED

50 G (1¾ OZ) FRESH HORSERADISH, PEELED

First make 2 thin omelettes. Melt half the butter in a non-stick frying pan until foaming. Pour in half the beaten eggs and cook for 2 minutes until just firm. Flip over and cook on the other side for 1 minute. Remove from the pan and repeat with the remaining eggs. Set aside on a chopping board. Cut each omelette in half to make 4 half-moons.

Combine the herring, diced onion, mayonnaise, dill and peas in a bowl.

Slice the baguette down the middle and line with the slices of omelette. Spoon in the herring mixture and top with the lettuce. Garnish with the onion slices, then using a zester, grate over the fresh horseradish. Cut the baguette into quarters and serve.

Hot-smoked salmon, roasted garlic & apple salad

Most of the smoked salmon that you buy in shops – the kind that is usually sold in flat slices – is cold smoked. This means it has been smoked for a long time without any heat source. I prefer hot-smoked salmon, which is usually sold as an individual fillet. The smoky flavour in hot-smoked salmon is bolder and it has a similar texture to cooked salmon. Like all smoked fish, hot-smoked salmon makes a great base for a salad because of its fantastic intense flavour and saltiness. Here, the roasted garlic yoghurt provides a much-needed savoury note, and the crisp apple provides sweetness and crunch.

SERVES 4

- 1 GARLIC BULB
- 250 G (9 OZ/1 CUP) NATURAL YOGHURT
- 100 ML (3½ FL OZ) FULL-CREAM (WHOLE) MILK
- PINCH OF WHITE PEPPER
- 500 G (1 LB 2 OZ) HOT-SMOKED SALMON (SEE PAGE 29)
- ½ RED ONION, THINLY SLICED
- ½ TELEGRAPH CUCUMBER, HALVED LENGTHWAYS AND THINLY SLICED
- ½ BUNCH RADISHES, THINLY SLICED INTO COLD WATER
- 1 GRANNY SMITH APPLE, CORED AND THINLY SLICED INTO ACIDULATED WATER
- 150 G (5½ OZ) WATERCRESS OR MÂCHE
- ½ LEMON

Preheat the oven to 200°C (400°F). Place the garlic on a baking tray and cook for 20–25 minutes, until the edges start to turn dark brown. Squeeze the garlic flesh into a bowl and mash with a fork. Add the yoghurt, milk and white pepper and mash together, making sure the garlic is evenly combined. Season, to taste.

Flake the salmon into a separate bowl and gently combine with the onion, cucumber, drained radish and apple slices and the watercress or mâche. Transfer to a serving platter and drizzle with the yoghurt sauce. Squeeze over the lemon and serve.

Any leftover yoghurt sauce will keep in the refrigerator for up to one week.

Rye tart with chard, roe & sunny-side eggs

This dish is perfect for plonking in the middle of the table. Just make sure your share has a bit with the oozy egg yolk and lots of salty exploding roe – delicious! If you find that the centre of the tart has lost too much moisture during baking, serve it together with the Roasted Garlic Yoghurt Dressing (page 126).

SERVES 6

600 G (1 LB 5 OZ) CHARD (OR A MIXTURE OF CHARD, SILVERBEET AND KALE), CHOPPED

2 TABLESPOONS OLIVE OIL

1 LEEK, MIDDLE-THIRD ONLY, THINLY SLICED

2 GARLIC CLOVES, FINELY SLICED

4–6 EGGS

4 TABLESPOONS SALMON ROE

TART BASE

210 G (7½ OZ/1⅓ CUPS) PLAIN WHITE FLOUR

140 G (5 OZ) FINE RYE FLOUR

170 G (6 OZ) BUTTER

A PINCH OF SALT

70 ML ICE-COLD WATER

For the tart base, combine the ingredients with the ice-cold water in the bowl of a stand mixer or food processor with the dough hook attachment added. Mix together to form a smooth dough, adding a little extra water if the dough is looking a little crumbly.

Pat the ball of dough to create an oval shape. Cover with plastic wrap and place in the refrigerator for 40 minutes to rest.

Preheat the oven to 180°C (350°F).

While the pastry is resting, cook the chard in batches. Heat a third of the olive oil in a large frying pan over a medium heat. Add a third of the chard, leek and garlic, season with salt and sauté for 4 minutes, or until wilting. Remove the mixture from the pan and set aside, then repeat the process twice more with the remaining chard, leek, garlic and oil. Set aside.

Take the pastry from the refrigerator, remove the top layer of plastic wrap and flip it over onto a sheet of baking paper. Wait 5 minutes for the dough to become workable, then, working quickly, roll it out into a rectangle approximately 20 cm x 35 cm (8 in x 14 in).

Spread the chard and leek mixture over the centre of the tart base, leaving a border of about 6 cm (2½ in) from the edges and leaving behind any moisture that may have leached from the wilted chard. Fold over the edges roughly and bake for 40 minutes. Crack over the eggs, return to the oven and bake for a further 5 minutes, until the eggwhites have just set. To serve, top with the roe and accompany with a simple green salad.

Iceberg smørrebrød with gravlax & ymerdrys

This recipe tips the idea of the typical Nordic open sandwich – or smørrebrød *– on its head, putting the wonderful texture of rye ymerdrys on salmon and lettuce rather than the other way around.*

SERVES 4

1 HANDFUL EACH OF DILL, CHERVIL AND PARSLEY, ROUGHLY CHOPPED OR TORN

2 TABLESPOONS CHOPPED CHIVES

JUICE OF ½ LIME

1 FIRM, COMPACT ICEBERG LETTUCE, TRIMMED AND OUTER LEAVES REMOVED

200 G (7 OZ) THINLY SLICED GRAVLAX OR SMOKED SALMON

PEA TENDRILS TO SERVE

YMERDRYS

200 G (7 OZ) AUTHENTIC WAXY DANISH RYE BREAD, BROKEN INTO LARGE CHUNKS

2 TABLESPOONS BROWN SUGAR

MUSTARD DRESSING

1 TEASPOON MILD AMERICAN-STYLE MUSTARD

3 TABLESPOONS PLAIN YOGHURT

½ TEASPOON HONEY (ONLY IF YOU ARE USING SMOKED SALMON, GRAVLAX IS SWEET ENOUGH)

Preheat the oven to 180°C (350°F). Line a baking tray with baking paper.

To make the *ymerdrys*, pulse the bread in a food processor, gradually adding the sugar, until the consistency resembles loose soil.

Spread the mixture out over the prepared baking tray and bake in the oven for 10–15 minutes, until it takes on a rich brown colour. Watch closely in the last 5 minutes to make sure it doesn't burn. Remove from the oven and allow to cool on the tray.

For the dressing, mix the mustard, yoghurt and honey, if using, together in a bowl.

In a separate bowl, mix together the herbs, chopped chives and lime juice.

Place the lettuce upright on a chopping board and cut vertically into 2.5 cm (1 in) rounds. Setting aside the outer pieces, transfer four of the central lettuce rounds to a serving plate.

To build your '*smørrebrød*', spread the dressing over the lettuce rounds, top with the gravlax or smoked salmon and spoon over the lime juice and herb mixture. Sprinkle over the *ymerdrys* and pea tendrils to serve.

Cod en papillote with green tomatoes & dill

This French technique of steaming is one of my favourite ways to cook fish. Anything can be encased in the paper to impart flavour – it's quick, healthy and creates little mess.

This year, whether the outcome of a poor summer or the result of planting them out too late, our tomatoes remained green. But in the true Nordic spirit of making the best of climate adversity we transformed them into these tart slithers, which serve to do the job of lemon and accompany the dill perfectly. Crown dill, the flower head of the dill herb, has a more liquorice and intense flavour than the leaves. If you can't find it you can replicate the flavour by using fresh dill and a very light dusting of liquorice root powder instead.

SERVES 2

2 X 150 G (5½ OZ) COD FILLETS OR OTHER FIRM WHITE FISH FILLETS

2 SMALL GREEN TOMATOES, THINLY SLICED INTO DISCS

20 G (¾ OZ) GREEN CABBAGE, ROUGHLY CHOPPED (OR OTHER GREENS SUCH AS ASPARAGUS OR LEEKS)

3 CROWN DILL HEADS OR DILL SPRIGS

PINCH OF LIQUORICE POWDER (IF USING DILL SPRIGS)

1 TEASPOON SMOKED OR REGULAR SEA SALT FLAKES

1 TEASPOON OLIVE OIL

Preheat the oven to 180°C (350°F). Fold a 40 cm x 30 cm (16 in x 12 in) sheet of baking paper in half. Cut off the corners to create round edges with scissors, then fold the baking paper out to give you a heart-shaped piece ready to cook with.

Place the fish in the centre of the prepared baking paper and top with the tomatoes, chopped cabbage and crown dill or dill sprigs and liquorice powder. Sprinkle over the sea salt and drizzle over the olive oil, then fold over the paper to form a parcel. Crimp the edges and twist the paper at both ends to seal the deal.

Place the parcel on a tray in the middle of the oven and bake for 12–15 minutes, or until cooked through.

Unwrap and eat straight from the paper or transfer to serving plates.

Brined cod, parsnip & *ymerdrys*

In this simple, well-rounded dish, the tenderised cod is gently poached. Sweetness from the sugared rye crumbs in the ymerdrys *pairs well with the earthy mushrooms, while the sorrel provides a necessary lemony kick.*

SERVES 4

2 X 350 G (12½ OZ) OR 4 X 175 G (6 OZ) COD FILLETS

2 TABLESPOONS YMERDRYS (SEE PAGE 53)

4 BUTTON MUSHROOMS, VERY THINLY SLICED (USE A MANDOLINE OR VEGETABLE PEELER)

BRINE

500 ML (17 FL OZ/2 CUPS) WARM WATER

1 TABLESPOON SALT

1 TABLESPOON CASTER (SUPERFINE) SUGAR

PARSNIP PURÉE

4 SMALL PARSNIPS, CUT INTO CHUNKY DISCS

1 LARGE POTATO, PEELED AND CUT INTO ROUGH 2 CM (¾ IN) CHUNKS

120 ML (4 FL OZ) FULL-CREAM (WHOLE) MILK

1 TABLESPOON SALTED BUTTER

HERB BUTTER

50 G (1¾ OZ) SALTED BUTTER

HANDFUL OF SORREL OR LEMON BALM LEAVES (SEE PAGE 297)

Mix together the brine ingredients in a large bowl until the sugar has dissolved, then soak the fish for 15 minutes.

Meanwhile, for the purée, boil the parsnips with the potato in salted water for about 15 minutes, until tender. Bring the milk to a simmer and then set aside.

Drain the parsnips and potato well, then blend with the butter and a little of the warm milk until totally smooth: the purée should be the consistency of double cream, so add more milk if necessary. Season, to taste, and keep warm.

Bring 1 litre (34 fl oz/4 cups) water to a simmer over a low heat. Remove the cod from the brine and gently rinse it with cold water before placing it in the simmering water with a slotted spoon. Cook for 4–5 minutes, until the flesh easily breaks away in the centre of the fillets when poked with a fork. Carefully transfer to a plate and cover with foil to keep warm.

For the herb butter gently heat the butter with the sorrel or lemon balm leaves in a non-stick saucepan. When the butter is foaming and has started to change colour, immediately remove the pan from the heat.

Divide the purée between serving plates (you can reheat it quickly if you need to). Top with the fish (breaking the fillets in half if you have used 2 larger ones), scatter over the *ymerdrys* and garnish with the slices of raw mushroom. Finally, pour over the browned herb butter.

Mackerel, buckwheat & pear salad

Salty and full of flavour, smoked fish is extremely versatile and perfect for the lead role in this salad. Smoked mackerel can be quite rich but here it is balanced by fresh, tart pear and crisp celery. Toasted buckwheat is an example of a new technique being applied to an old ingredient – one of the tenets of new Nordic cooking. It provides a great texture and an earthy savoury note. The mustard dressing is a staple, and goes very well with any seafood that is a bit more robust.

SERVES 4

2 TABLESPOONS WHOLEGRAIN BUCKWHEAT

150–200 G (5½–7 OZ) SMOKED MACKEREL FILLET

½ RED ONION, THINLY SLICED

1 CELERY HEART, THINLY SLICED

1 NASHI OR YOUNG TART ACIDIC PEAR, CORED AND THINLY SLICED INTO ACIDULATED WATER

MUSTARD DILL SAUCE (SEE PAGE 43), TO SERVE

DILL SPRIGS, TO GARNISH

Preheat the oven to 170°C (340°F). Spread the buckwheat on a baking tray and cook in the oven for 10–15 minutes, until it turns golden brown – don't let it burn. To test if it is ready, bite on a piece; it should still be quite firm but should not break your teeth!

Flake the fish into a large serving bowl. Add the onion, celery and drained pear and mix gently to combine.

Divide the salad between serving dishes, spoon over the mustard dill sauce and garnish with the toasted buckwheat and dill sprigs.

Scallops, porridge & radish

Earthy flavours play an important role in many new Nordic dishes. In this dish, the scallops and spelt provide a wonderful contrast that really accentuates their unique flavours. Crisp, fresh radish finishes off the dish with a satisfying crunch and peppery punch. If you'd like a little extra saltiness, garnish with a little fish roe.

SERVES 4

2 TABLESPOONS OLIVE OIL

50 G (1¾ OZ) THIN SLICES OF PROSCIUTTO, OR PIECE OF SPECK, CHOPPED INTO STRIPS

500 ML (17 FL OZ/2 CUPS) FISH STOCK

125 G (4½ OZ) ROLLED SPELT FLAKES

1 TEASPOON APPLE CIDER VINEGAR

1 TABLESPOON SALTED BUTTER

12 SCALLOPS

1 TABLESPOON CHOPPED DILL

150 G (5½ OZ) RADISHES, JULIENNED AND SUBMERGED IN COLD WATER

LEMON OR LIME WEDGES, TO SERVE (OPTIONAL)

Heat 1 tablespoon of the olive oil in a frying pan and cook the prosciutto for 3–4 minutes, until crisp. Drain on paper towel.

Pour the stock and 200 ml (7 fl oz) water into a saucepan and bring to a simmer over a medium heat. Add the spelt flakes and cook, stirring often, until it has the consistency of wet porridge. This will take 8–10 minutes. Remove from the heat. Stir through the vinegar, check the seasoning and set the pan aside.

In a clean non-stick frying pan heat the remaining oil and the butter over a high heat. When the butter is foaming, fry the scallops for 1–1½ minutes on each side until just cooked.

Stir the prosciutto and dill through the porridge. If the porridge has become a bit claggy and gluey, add a little boiling water to loosen it.

Spoon the porridge into serving bowls and top with the scallops and drained radishes. Serve with lemon or lime wedges for squeezing, if desired.

Flounder & Nordic bread salad

Given that bread is so popular in all Nordic countries, it felt only right to develop a bread salad. This one makes a great accompaniment to all seafood. Really, any fish will work here – a whole roasted snapper or sea bream are both excellent choices – but I love the delicate flesh of flounder. It is also very easy to cook and share across the table. Flounder is commonly found in the shallows of Nordic seas and, for the first time in this chapter, it's prepared as most fish usually is: in a pan! Flounder can also be found very easily at a quality fishmonger.

SERVES 4

60 G (2 OZ) PLAIN (ALL-PURPOSE) FLOUR

1 TEASPOON SALT

1 TEASPOON WHITE PEPPER

1 OR 2 WHOLE FLOUNDERS, DEPENDING ON SIZE (YOU WILL NEED AT LEAST 1 KG/2 LB 3 OZ)

25 G (1 OZ) SALTED BUTTER

1 TABLESPOON RAPESEED OIL

SALAD

200 G (7 OZ) RYE BREAD (SEE PAGES 231–33)

½ RED ONION, THINLY SLICED

PINCH OF WHITE PEPPER

50 ML (1¾ FL OZ) APPLE CIDER VINEGAR

1 TEASPOON SOFT BROWN SUGAR

2 TABLESPOONS OLIVE OIL

200 G (7 OZ) RADISHES, THINLY SLICED

1 TABLESPOON RINSED CAPERS

6 MEDITERRANEAN ANCHOVIES IN OIL, THINLY SLICED LENGTHWAYS, OR 4 PIECES OF PICKLED HERRING, VERY FINELY DICED

½ TELEGRAPH CUCUMBER, PEELED IF PREFERRED, THINLY SLICED

2 TABLESPOONS CHOPPED DILL

For the salad, tear the bread into rough 3 cm (1¼ in) pieces and put it in a bowl. Add the onion and season with salt and white pepper.

Combine the vinegar and sugar until the sugar has dissolved, then mix in the olive oil. Toss through the bread onion until evenly coated, then set aside.

Season the flour with the salt and white pepper. Lightly dust each side of the fish. Heat the butter and rapeseed oil in a frying pan over a medium heat until the butter is foaming. Fry the fish for about 5 minutes on each side, depending on its size. To test if it is cooked, use a knife to lift away some of the flesh at its thickest point; if it comes away easily, it is ready.

Add the remaining ingredients to the bread salad, mix together and serve alongside the fish.

Cod, cabbage & smoked rye

Cod is a funny one. It is highly prized around the world, but someone snacking on a delicate coral trout or garfish may wonder what all the fuss is about. Cooked badly, it can be rubbery and bland. Personally, the jury is still out, but I have to say it is hard to beat perfectly cooked skrei, *the highest grade of cod, when it is first available in January having been rushed down from the Barents Sea to Norway.*

Still, whatever you think of it, this popular fish has had a long and eventful history, from the start of its international trade during the Viking era, right up to the recent cod wars between Iceland and England. Many countries, including Portugal and Italy, drool over the air-dried and salted cod fillet – a form that I also adore. This recipe draws influence from that famous salty dried cod preparation, known as stockfish, bacalao *or* brandade, *but adapted here for a fresh fillet.*

The recipe also gives instructions for smoking the bread. If you don't have a smoker, you can re-create a similar flavour using hickory smoke powder.

SERVES 4

200 G (7 OZ) RED CABBAGE, FINELY SHREDDED

200 ML (7 FL OZ) STRONG PICKLING SOLUTION (SEE PAGE 34)

800 G (1 LB 12 OZ) POTATOES, PEELED

500 ML (17 FL OZ/2 CUPS) FULL-CREAM (WHOLE) MILK

1 BAY LEAF

PINCH OF WHITE PEPPER

4 MEDITERRANEAN ANCHOVIES IN OIL, FINELY CHOPPED, PLUS 2 TEASPOONS OF THE OIL

600 G (1 LB 5 OZ) COD FILLETS

1 TABLESPOON SALTED BUTTER

JUICE OF ¼ LEMON

SMOKED RYE

200 G (7 OZ) RYE BREAD (SEE PAGES 231–3)

1 TEASPOON HICKORY SMOKE POWDER (IF NOT SMOKING THE BREAD) ALONG WITH 25 G (1 OZ) SALTED BUTTER

If you are going to smoke the bread, do that first. Cut the rye bread into very thin slices and place in a smoker for 20 minutes.

Meanwhile, pickle the cabbage in the pickling solution, and boil the potatoes in a large saucepan of salted water for 12–15 minutes, until soft. Drain well.

While the potatoes are cooking, combine the milk, bay leaf, white pepper, anchovies and anchovy oil in a large saucepan. Heat gently for 4–5 minutes, until the milk is steaming but not simmering. Add the cod in a single layer; the fish should be fully submerged in the milk. If you have a kitchen thermometer, the temperature should be around 60°C (140°F), but no hotter. Cook for 4 minutes, then turn over the fillets. Cook for a further 5 minutes, depending on the thickness of the fish; it should break apart when prodded with a fork. Remove from the heat. Gently lift the cod from the milk and set aside on a plate. Pour half the milk into a jug, leaving the rest in the pan, discarding the bay leaf.

If you don't have a smoker, preheat the oven to 180°C (350°F), sprinkle hickory smoke powder on to thinly sliced buttered rye bread and cook for about 5 minutes, until the bread has dried out, and is golden at the edges and crisp.

Add the drained potatoes to the milk mixture in the pan and mash together with the butter. It should have the consistency of dense mash; if it's too thick add some more of the warm milk from the jug. Flake in the cod and stir through. Taste and adjust the seasoning with salt and lemon juice.

Spoon the mash into serving bowls, top with pickled cabbage and torn slices of rye.

kärlek
Pale Ale

Salmon carpaccio & cucumber waldorf

I like to keep a large salmon fillet in the freezer like this – it makes for easy slicing whenever you want beautifully thin strips for a carpaccio, while the act of freezing also kills off any parasites that can be found in this naturally oily fish. To avoid the salmon's flavour being tainted by other products in the freezer, be sure to keep it stored in a zip-lock bag.

The salmon slices here are very versatile and can be used with a variety of salad and dressing combinations, while the salad itself can be used to accompany many dishes. If you prefer your salmon less raw, give it a more solid hit of citrus and it will develop more of a cooked profile through a little maceration.

SERVES 2 WITH LEFTOVERS

1 X 800 G (1 LB 12 OZ) SUPER-FRESH SKIN-ON SALMON FILLET, SEALED IN A ZIP-LOCK BAG AND FROZEN (IT'S BEST TO BUY A LARGER FILLET AND LEAVE IT IN THE FREEZER FOR MULTIPLE OCCASIONS)

1 TABLESPOON EXTRA-VIRGIN OLIVE OIL

LIME WEDGES TO SERVE

REDWOOD SORREL LEAVES TO GARNISH

CUCUMBER WALDORF

1 HANDFUL GREEN GRAPES, HALVED

½ CUCUMBER, PEELED AND THINLY SLICED ON A MANDOLINE

40 G (1½ OZ) WALNUTS, ROUGHLY CHOPPED

1 CELERY STALK, THINLY SLICED ON AN ANGLE

½ GRANNY SMITH APPLE, CORED AND THINLY SLICED ON A MANDOLINE

DRESSING

1 TEASPOON DIJON MUSTARD

125 G (4½ OZ) PLAIN YOGHURT

A SQUEEZE OF LEMON JUICE

1 TEASPOON OLIVE OIL

1½ TEASPOONS SEA SALT FLAKES

Remove the salmon from the freezer and leave it to thaw a little on a clean work surface for 15 minutes.

Meanwhile, mix together the dressing ingredients in a bowl until well combined.

For the cucumber waldorf, put all the ingredients in a large bowl. Add the dressing and toss together well.

Now, back to the salmon. Using a very sharp knife, and starting at the narrow end of the fillet, slice it into very thin slices on a 45° angle (this will give each slice the maximum amount of surface area). Plate each slice as you go, fanning the slices out side by side to cover two serving plates. Return the remaining salmon fillet to the zip-lock bag and freezer.

To serve, pile the salad over the centre of each plate, drizzle over the olive oil and squeeze over as much lime juice as you like. Garnish with redwood sorrel leaves.

CHAPTER FIVE

From the Farm

Rocky soil and dense forest have made grazing land a scarce resource in Nordic countries. In fact, a large chunk of the population emigrated to the Americas for this very reason. That said, the majority of the meat that is produced is of the highest quality and demand is strong. Lamb and beef come with a bit of a hefty price tag, but pork, easily the most consumed meat, is more affordable.

Rather than meat being the central ingredient around which all others revolve, it is the whole grains and cold-climate vegetables that are attracting the attention of contemporary chefs; meat is assuming a more supportive role. This willingness to explore innovative ways of working with ingredients is what I love the most about new Nordic cuisine. And nowhere, perhaps, is this better expressed, than in the clever and unusual use of vegetables. In this way, the land – both the animals that live on it and the plants that grow in it – are celebrated at the new Nordic table.

A note worth making before we get into the recipes is that Nordic countries have an unexpected and mildly perplexing infatuation with hot dogs! They are the most common snack food across the entire region. Roadside stands are everywhere. Classic toppings include tomato sauce (ketchup), mustard and fried shallots, but there are also some more surprising ones to try, such as prawn (shrimp) and mayonnaise salad, and Boston gurka, an incredibly sweet mix of finely chopped gherkins and raw onion. And in regional Finland, forget the bread: it's just a fat smoked pork sausage served with some paper wrapped around and as much sweet mustard as you can handle.

The chapter ahead introduces us to some more modern vegetable and meat dishes using traditional Nordic ingredients.

Beetroot, goat's cheese, pea relish & cocoa nibs

I love being surprised by new uses for well-known ingredients or unusual food combinations. Not everything works, but the spirit is alive for change! In this recipe, the bitterness and crunch of the cocoa nibs contrasts well with the sweet beetroots (beets). Served as a carpaccio, it's a great looking starter.

SERVES 4

600 G (1 LB 5 OZ) FRESH BEETROOT (BEETS), PEELED AND LEFT WHOLE

400 ML (13½ FL OZ) MULLED OR SWEET RED WINE COMBINED WITH 1 TABLESPOON OF MIXED GROUND CHRISTMAS SPICES, SUCH AS STAR ANISE, CARDAMOM AND CINNAMON

1 TEASPOON SALT

½ RED ONION, FINELY DICED

1 TABLESPOON RAPESEED OIL

2 TEASPOONS CIDER VINEGAR

2 TEASPOONS CASTER (SUPERFINE) SUGAR

125 G (4½ OZ/1 CUP) PEAS, FRESH OR THAWED IF FROZEN

150 G (5½ OZ) GOAT'S CHEESE

1 TABLESPOON CRUSHED COCOA NIBS

FRESH LEMON BALM OR MINT LEAVES, TO SERVE

2 TABLESPOONS ALMOND OR HAZELNUT OIL

In a covered saucepan, simmer the beetroot in the wine, 600 ml (20½ fl oz) water and salt over a low heat for about 50 minutes. When they are ready, a knife should pass through them easily; if they're not soft enough cook them for a little longer. Drain and allow to cool.

While they are cooling, sauté the onion in the rapeseed oil over a low heat for about 4 minutes, until translucent – do not let it colour. Increase the heat and stir in the vinegar, sugar and peas. Cook for 1 minute, then remove from the heat. Use a fork to mash the mixture together then allow to cool in the refrigerator.

Using a mandoline, peeler or a sharp knife, slice the beetroots into thin discs and arrange over serving plates. Top with the pea relish and crumble over the cheese. Scatter with the cocoa nibs and herbs and drizzle with the almond or hazelnut oil.

Chilled pea & dill soup with rye

Memories of hot summer days are not plentiful in Nordic parts! Still, when they do happen, these beautiful days are unforgettable. I remember eating this deliciously refreshing chilled soup in the middle of July while sitting underneath a tree, with plenty of sourdough bread to dip in. It's a very easy soup to make, especially if you are happy using frozen peas – just make sure they are the best quality you can find.

It may seem a little odd to use sugar in the garnish, but it acts as a 'cure' for the leek and is well worth trying. You can use the same method with red onion; it draws out the moisture and takes away some of the bitterness.

SERVES 4

400 G (14 OZ) PEAS

1 SMALL LEEK (ABOUT 300 G/10½ OZ), GREEN PART FOR THE GARNISH, WHITE PART FOR COOKING

JUICE OF ½ LEMON

1 TEASPOON CASTER (SUPERFINE) SUGAR

6 SLICES RYE BREAD (SEE PAGES 231–33), CUT INTO 2 CM (¾ IN) CUBES

2 TABLESPOONS SALTED BUTTER

2 TABLESPOONS RAPESEED OIL

1 GARLIC CLOVE, CHOPPED

2 SMALL CELERY STALKS, FINELY DICED

1 TABLESPOON NATURAL YOGHURT

500 ML (17 FL OZ/2 CUPS) COLD CHICKEN STOCK (MAKE SURE THERE IS LITTLE TO NO FAT)

PINCH OF WHITE PEPPER

2 TABLESPOONS CHOPPED DILL, PLUS MORE TO GARNISH IF YOU LIKE

ICE CUBES (OPTIONAL)

If you're using fresh peas, boil them for 2 minutes then drain and rinse in cold water. If using frozen peas, rinse them and let them defrost.

Thinly slice the green part of the leek for the garnish and combine with the lemon juice and sugar in a bowl. Set aside.

Sauté the rye bread in the butter and 1 tablespoon of the oil over a low heat for about 5 minutes, until golden brown. Tip on to paper towel and allow to cool.

Finely chop the white part of the leek and add to the pan with the remaining oil and the garlic and celery. Sauté over a medium heat for 4 minutes, until soft and translucent. Transfer to a blender.

Reserving 50 g (1¾ oz) of the peas for a garnish, tip the rest of the peas into the blender with the leek, garlic and celery. Add the yoghurt and stock and season well with salt and white pepper. Blend for 1 minute, then check the seasoning. Add the dill and blend for about 30 seconds more, until it has a thin, aerated consistency.

If the soup isn't cold, place a few ice cubes in each bowl before serving. Divide the soup among the serving bowls, spoon a little leek on top and garnish with the reserved peas and rye croutons. Sprinkle over more dill if you like.

keller

Veggie chips with horseradish cream & bottarga

Although bottarga is essentially a Mediterranean product, the compressed salted fish roe has a yeasty, salty, fishy flavour that is very Scandinavian. Like most products of this nature it's important to use it sparingly and balance it with other flavours. Speaking of which, while I know deep-frying is not a healthy way of cooking – even if it is root veggies – sometimes exceptions have to be made.

SERVES 8

Peel the veggies then slice them very thinly into long strips using a mandoline.

Half-fill a large heavy-based saucepan or fryer with oil and heat until the temperature reaches 180°C (350°F), or until a cube of bread browns in 30 seconds.

Carefully lower the veggies into the hot oil in batches and fry for 3–4 minutes, turning halfway during cooking, until the veggies are floating on the surface of the oil and the bubbling has reduced to almost nil. Transfer to paper towel to drain off the excess oil and sprinkle generously with sea salt.

Put the horseradish cream in a shallow dish and place the bottarga in a separate bowl or small jar for the guests to add at will. Serve the veggie chips alongside the horseradish cream for dipping. If you find the chips crack under the weight of the cream, then simply spoon a little on top of each chip.

2 PARSNIPS

2 CARROTS

2 BEETROOT (BEETS)

1 SWEET POTATO

2 POTATOES

SUNFLOWER OIL, FOR DEEP-FRYING

SEA SALT FLAKES

250 G (9 OZ/1½ CUPS) HORSERADISH CREAM

2 TEASPOONS GRATED BOTTARGA

Baked cauliflower & juniper soup

The lesser-practised technique of roasting cauliflower whole brings out a distinctly different flavour, one that is nutty and more caramel-like. It is enhanced in this recipe by brown butter and fragrant juniper. Adding the cream is optional. Enjoy with some rye bread (see pages 231–33) or buttered crispbread on a cold day.

SERVES 4

4 DRIED JUNIPER BERRIES

1 TABLESPOON FLAKED SALT

600 G (1 LB 5 OZ) WHOLE CAULIFLOWER

1 TABLESPOON RAPESEED OIL

AROUND 600 ML (20½ FL OZ) CHICKEN STOCK

50 G (1¾ OZ) BROWN BUTTER (PAGE 46)

100 G (3½ OZ) CRÈME FRAÎCHE OR SOUR CREAM (OPTIONAL)

PINCH OF WHITE PEPPER

RYE BREAD (SEE PAGES 231–33) OR SEEDY CRISPBREADS (PAGE 227), TO SERVE

Preheat the oven to 200°C (400°F). Using a mortar and pestle, grind the juniper berries with the salt.

Remove most of the leaves from the cauliflower, keeping a few around the base. Rub the juniper berry mixture and the oil over the cauliflower. Place on a baking tray and roast in the oven for 40 minutes, or until golden brown all over. Check that it's cooked through by piercing the thicker stems with a sharp knife; they should be tender. If it's not quite ready, reduce the temperature to 170°C (340°F) and cook for a little longer.

Remove from the oven and break apart the florets, reserving the thinner leaves for a garnish.

Heat the chicken stock, then blend the cauliflower, adding the stock gradually. It should have a fairly thick consistency, so you may not need all the stock.

Add the brown butter, crème fraîche or sour cream (if using) and a pinch of white pepper, and blend again. Check the seasoning before serving with bread and garnish with the reserved leaves.

Potted trout with pickled fennel on rye

Fennel is a very popular ingredient across all Nordic countries and I love its strong anise flavour. Although originating from the Mediterranean, it is a winter vegetable that grows happily this far north. Trout rivers can be found inland almost anywhere you travel in the region, and the fly-fishing culture is strong. In this recipe, I have used a slightly more conventional preparation method, perhaps closer to the classical French or English styles, which sits well alongside the multitude of traditional Nordic preservation techniques. The natural sweetness of the butter and fish is a great match for the slightly sour rye bread. Ask your fishmonger to gut the fish for you.

SERVES 6

1 X 700 G (1 LB 9 OZ) WHOLE TROUT (YOU WILL NEED 500 G/1 LB 2 OZ FLESH AFTER COOKING)

250 G (9 OZ) UNSALTED BUTTER

1 GARLIC CLOVE, FINELY GRATED

PINCH OF WHITE PEPPER

1 TEASPOON GROUND FENNEL SEEDS

FINELY GRATED ZEST OF 1 LEMON

1 TEASPOON VERY FINELY CHOPPED THYME LEAVES

RYE BREAD (SEE PAGES 231–33) OR SOURDOUGH, TO SERVE

1 FENNEL BULB, VERY THINLY SLICED AND LIGHTLY PICKLED (SEE PAGE 34)

RADISHES, THINLY SLICED INTO COLD WATER, TO SERVE

DILL FRONDS, TO GARNISH

Sterilise a glass jar by washing it thoroughly in hot soapy water, rinsing well, then putting it on a baking tray in a low oven (120°C/250°F) for 20 minutes. Leave to cool.

Preheat the oven to 180°C (350°F). Salt the inside of the trout and wrap it loosely in foil, sealing it like an envelope. Cook in the oven for 12–15 minutes. To check for doneness, open the foil and use a fork to pull the flesh away from the bones. If it comes away easily and there is no translucent flesh, it is ready. Flake off all the flesh and set aside.

Meanwhile, clarify the butter by melting it in a small saucepan over a low heat until the white solids separate out. Gently pour the golden melted butter into a frying pan and discard the solids.

Warm the clarified butter then add the garlic, white pepper and fennel seeds. Sizzle gently for 1–2 minutes then remove the frying pan from the heat and add the lemon zest and thyme. Stir for a few seconds, then add a pinch of salt.

Spread out the trout on a plate, trickle over four-fifths of the spiced butter and mix together gently. Spoon the mixture into the sterilised jar, packing it in firmly and ensuring there are no air pockets.

Pour the remaining spiced butter on top to seal the mixture. Chill in the refrigerator for at least a day to set. (It can be kept in the refrigerator for up to a week.)

To serve, remove from the refrigerator 20 minutes before eating, spread the trout on slices of rye bread (toasted, if you like) and top with pickled fennel, drained radish slices and dill.

Onion & cider soup

Sweet, soft onions are so underrated! The bitter taste from charring the onions and the yeasty cider are welcome additions to this classic soup.

SERVES 6

In a large heavy-based saucepan, sauté the sliced onions in the butter over a low–medium heat until soft and brown – this can take up to 45 minutes, lowering the heat towards the end. Add the cider to deglaze the pan, then add the salt and stock, bring to a simmer and cook, covered, for 30 minutes.

Meanwhile, heat a chargrill pan or cast-iron frying pan until almost smoking. Turn your ventilation up as high as possible or open your window, as this will get quite smoky. Halve the remaining whole onion, leaving the skin intact, and place the halves, cut side down, in the pan. Cook for 5–8 minutes, or until the flesh is blackened and charred and the centre of the onion is soft. Remove the onion from the pan and leave to cool, then peel off the skin and separate the onion layers into petals.

To serve, divide the soup between serving bowls, top each with a few of the onion petals and garnish with a few tarragon sprigs.

1KG (2 LB 4 OZ) ONIONS, HALVED AND THINLY SLICED, PLUS 1 EXTRA WHOLE ONION

150 G (5½ OZ) UNSALTED BUTTER, CUT INTO CUBES

375 ML (13 FL OZ/1½ CUPS) DRY CIDER

1½ TEASPOONS SEA SALT

1.5 LITRES (54 FL OZ/6 CUPS) VEGETABLE STOCK

TARRAGON SPRIGS TO GARNISH

Baked pointed cabbage, beluga lentils & smoked cheese

It's great that high-end restaurants are now offering up things like cabbage wedges as a main course. That was un-imaginable in the past. Pointed cabbage, also known as hispi or sweetheart cabbage, is a sweet, soft cabbage perfect for roasting. This can be eaten as a main or served as a side to meat dishes.

SERVES 6

3 DRIED JUNIPER BERRIES

1 TEASPOON SALT

2 X 500 G (1 LB 2 OZ) POINTED CABBAGE HEADS, EACH CUT INTO 4 WEDGES

2 TABLESPOONS RAPESEED OIL

LENTILS

200 G (7 OZ/1 CUP) DRIED BELUGA (SMALL BLACK) LENTILS, RINSED

1 TEASPOON SALT

1 TABLESPOON EXTRA-VIRGIN OLIVE OIL

3 SHALLOTS, FINELY DICED

2 TABLESPOONS BEST-QUALITY BALSAMIC, SHERRY OR RASPBERRY VINEGAR

SMOKED CHEESE SAUCE

20 G (¾ OZ) SALTED BUTTER

20 G (¾ OZ) PLAIN (ALL-PURPOSE) FLOUR

500 ML (18 FL OZ/2 CUPS) MILK

100 G (3½ OZ) SMOKED CHEESE SUCH AS GOUDA OR CHEDDAR

Preheat the oven to 200°C (400°F).

Crush the juniper berries together with the salt in a pestle and mortar. Arrange the cabbage wedges on a baking tray, brush with the oil and sprinkle over the juniper–salt mix. Roast the cabbage wedges in the oven for 30 minutes, turning them over 20 minutes into cooking.

While the cabbage is roasting, prepare the lentils and the smoked cheese sauce. Add the lentils to a saucepan together with the salt and 500 ml (18 fl oz/2 cups) of cold water, bring to a boil and cook for 20 minutes until soft (I like them nutty and al dente, but if you prefer them cooked more, add a little water towards the end and cook a little longer). Drain and return to the pan together with the oil and shallots. Stir through the vinegar, cover with a lid and keep warm.

For the cheese sauce, combine the butter and flour in a separate heavy-based saucepan over a low heat, to form a roux. Whisk in the milk and continue to cook over a low simmer, whisking all the while, for 8–10 minutes, or until the sauce has thickened. Stir through the cheese and set aside.

Once the cabbage has cooked for 30 minutes, remove it from the oven and spoon over half of the cheese sauce. Return to the oven and cook for a further 10 minutes, until the sauce is lightly golden in places.

Remove the wedges from the oven and arrange on a serving platter. Top with a generous scattering of the lentils and serve with bowls of the lentils and cheese sauce for extra helpings.

Whole celeriac, whole tarragon chicken & apple

The willingness of new Nordic chefs to explore different techniques for cooking common ingredients is something to admire. I have always eaten celeriac paired with potato in a purée and have considered it, at times, too powerful for my palate. In this recipe, it is roasted whole, which has the effect of softening and sweetening the flavours, while the nuttiness of the brown butter brings an interesting extra depth.

SERVES 4

80 G (2¾ OZ/1½ CUPS) PINE NUTS

1 X 1.5 KG (3 LB 5 OZ) CHICKEN

25 G (1 OZ) FRESH TARRAGON, LEAVES PICKED

WHITE PEPPER

1 TABLESPOON RAPESEED OIL

400 G (14 OZ) ASPARAGUS, WOODY ENDS REMOVED, THINLY SLICED AND LIGHTLY PICKLED (SEE PAGE 34)

RHUBARB CHUTNEY (PAGE 49), TO SERVE

ROASTED CELERIAC

1 X 600 G–1 KG (1 LB 5 OZ–2 LB 3 OZ) WHOLE CELERIAC, PEELED

50 G (1¾ OZ) BROWN BUTTER (PAGE 46), COOLED

3 DRIED JUNIPER BERRIES, GROUND

SALAD

150 G (5½ OZ) MÂCHE (BABY SPINACH OR ROCKET/ARUGULA ARE GOOD ALTERNATIVES)

1 GRANNY SMITH APPLE, THINLY SLICED INTO ACIDULATED WATER

DRESSING

1 TABLESPOON WHOLEGRAIN MUSTARD

100 ML (3½ FL OZ) OLIVE OIL

1 TABLESPOON APPLE CIDER VINEGAR

Preheat the oven to 150°C (300°F). Toast the pine nuts on a small baking tray for 5–10 minutes, until they are lightly golden. Shake the tray from time to time and don't let them burn. Transfer the pine nuts to a plate and set aside. Turn up the oven temperature to 180°F (350°F).

For the roasted celeriac, place the celeriac on a large sheet of foil and rub all over with the cold brown butter. Sprinkle with the ground juniper berries and some salt. Pierce the celeriac all over using a fork then wrap tightly in the foil, using an extra piece if required. Cook in the oven for 1½ hours, until it is soft all the way through when pierced with a knife. If you have a particularly large celeriac, it may take a little longer.

Once the celeriac is in the oven, prepare the chicken. Using your thumb and a spoon lift the skin from the chicken at the cavity end. Slide in half the tarragon leaves as far as you can then press the skin back down. Put the remaining leaves inside the cavity. Season the chicken with salt and white pepper and rub with the rapeseed oil. Tie the legs together with kitchen string then place in a roasting tray or casserole dish. Cook in the oven for 1 hour–1 hour 20 minutes. Check whether the chicken is cooked by piercing the flesh under the drumstick with a knife; if the juices run clear then it is ready.

Combine the mâche and drained apple in a bowl. Whisk together the ingredients for the dressing and toss with the salad.

Let the celeriac cool a little then use your hands to tear it into rough pieces. Top with the pickled asparagus and pine nuts, and serve alongside the chicken and mâche salad with some rhubarb chutney on the side.

Pork, barley & beetroot salad

The isterband sausage is a coarse, lightly smoked sausage from Småland in Sweden. It is made from pork, barley and potato and, eaten on its own, it can have quite an acidic taste. It is almost always served with pickled beetroot (beets) and dill potatoes. This salad uses those traditional components but distributes them in a different way throughout the dish.

SERVES 4

220 G (8 OZ/1 CUP) PEARL BARLEY

1 TABLESPOON APPLE CIDER VINEGAR

2 TABLESPOONS OLIVE OIL

600 G (1 LB 5 OZ) LIGHTLY SMOKED PORK SAUSAGES

1 TABLESPOON RAPESEED OIL

25 G (1 OZ) DILL FRONDS

100 G (3½ OZ) PICKLED BEETROOT (BEETS) (SEE PAGE 34)

2 ONIONS, CUT INTO 1 CM (½ IN) THICK RINGS

NATURAL YOGHURT, TO SERVE (OPTIONAL)

Soak the barley in 1 litre (34 fl oz/4 cups) water for 10 minutes. Drain and then boil in at least 4 litres (135 fl oz/16 cups) water for about 50 minutes. It should be slightly al dente. Drain, rinse briefly in cold water and drain again. Tip into a serving bowl and leave to cool for a few minutes, then stir through the vinegar and olive oil.

Fry the sausages in the rapeseed oil in a frying pan over a medium heat until cooked through. How long they take will depend on how thick the sausages are but they should be done in 10–12 minutes.

Slice the sausages on an angle into roughly 2 cm (¾ in) thick pieces. Mix through the barley with the dill and beetroot. Season to taste.

Preheat a chargrill pan to high and char the onion rings for about 2 minutes on each side until they are almost black. Add to the warm salad. Serve immediately with some yoghurt on the side, if desired.

Grilled cos, pear, cottage cheese & sunflower pesto

The grilled cos lettuce gives this dish a unique, pleasant flavour and texture, although you don't have to grill it if you don't want to. I like to make a batch of this pesto up and keep it for other dishes – unfortunately the sunflower kernels turn the pesto bitter if they are not soaked, so you'll need to start preparing this a day before eating.

SERVES 2 WITH LEFTOVERS

4 BABY COS (ROMAINE) LETTUCES, HALVED LENGTHWAYS

1 TABLESPOON RAPESEED OIL

2 CRISP NASHI OR BOSC PEARS, CORED AND THINLY SLICED INTO ACIDULATED COLD WATER

200 G (7 OZ) COTTAGE CHEESE

SUNFLOWER PESTO

125 G (4½ OZ/1 CUP) SUNFLOWER KERNELS, RINSED

2 GARLIC CLOVES

50 G (1¾ OZ) BABY SPINACH LEAVES

1 BUNCH BASIL, LEAVES ONLY

100 ML (3½ FL OZ) RAPESEED OIL

1 TEASPOON HONEY

100 G (3½ OZ) HARD, GRANULAR CHEESE (SUCH AS VÄSTERBOTTEN OR PARMESAN), GRATED

JUICE OF 1 LIME

To make the pesto, place the rinsed sunflower kernels in a small bowl or jar and pour over enough cold water to cover. Cover with plastic wrap and leave to soak overnight at room temperature.

Drain and rinse the sunflower kernels, then place them in a food processor or blender together with the garlic, spinach, basil, oil, honey, cheese and lime juice and blitz until all the ingredients have come together to form a rough paste. Season with salt to taste. If the pesto is a little too thick, thin it with a tablespoon or two of water.

Heat a chargrill pan until almost smoking. Brush the lettuce halves with the rapeseed oil, add to the pan, cut side down, and cook for 2 minutes, or until nicely charred.

Divide the lettuce halves between serving plates, top with the pear slices and spoon over the cottage cheese and dollops of the sunflower pesto to serve.

Beetroot, smoky cucumber & seedy crispbread

Smoking foods is a tricky procedure best left to restaurant chefs, or for when you happen to be taking a sojourn at a Scandinavian summer house, where outdoor smokers are commonplace. However, using smoked salt like this can impart a little of that same smoky flavour to the cucumber in this recipe quite easily.

You'll have some left-over beetroot here – these can be used to make beetroot crispbreads, blended into a cold beetroot gazpacho or used to make a beautiful salad with goat's cheese, toasted nuts and greens.

SERVES 2 WITH LEFTOVERS

700 G (1 LB 9 OZ) WHOLE BEETROOT (BEETS)

½ TELEGRAPH (LONG) CUCUMBER

1 TABLESPOON SMOKED SALT

3 TABLESPOONS HORSERADISH & APPLE YOGHURT DRESSING (BELOW)

50 G (1¾ OZ) SEEDY CRISPBREAD (PAGE 227), BROKEN INTO SHARDS

HORSERADISH & APPLE YOGHURT DRESSING

1 GRANNY SMITH APPLE

250 G (9 OZ/1 CUP) PLAIN YOGHURT

1 TABLESPOON FRESHLY GRATED HORSERADISH (OR FROM A JAR)

¼ TEASPOON SALT

Bring a large saucepan of salted water to the boil. Add the beetroot, cover and cook for 40 minutes, or until a paring knife passes through the centre easily.

Meanwhile, using a mandoline, shave the cucumber into long thin strips into a bowl. Add the smoked salt, toss through and leave for 5 minutes. Then add 1 litre (36 fl oz) of water. Set aside for 10 minutes, then drain.

When the beetroot are cooked, drain and refresh them under cold running water or in a bowl of iced water for 1 minute. Keeping one or two of the beetroot out for the salad, set aside the remainder in the refrigerator for another meal. Peel off the skins of the reserved beetroot and cut them into thin discs with the mandoline. Place the beetroot discs into a bowl.

To make the yoghurt dressing, peel and core the apple, then add to a food processor together with the remaining ingredients. Blitz together briefly to combine.

Add the yoghurt dressing to the beetroot discs and sprinkle with sea salt. Toss to combine.

Remove the cucumber pieces from the water and arrange on serving plates together with the beetroot. Scatter over the seedy crispbread shards to serve.

Smoked chicken, mustard yoghurt & poppy seeds

This sweet mustard yoghurt dressing is extremely versatile and goes well with pretty much everything. It is particularly compatible with the smoked chicken in this recipe. Poppy seeds are very popular in Nordic cuisine and breads are often sprinkled with them. A famous crispbread is covered with less-common white poppy seeds and legend tells it that these crispbreads were later banned from prisons because inmates tried to get a kick from them! As well as being a great combination of flavours and textures, this salad is also an example of the ease with which you can make Nordic dishes from what is already in your refrigerator. Sure, you may not have smoked chicken on hand but it's easy enough to find (or you could even make some yourself).

SERVES 4

100 G (3½ OZ) FRESH BABY SPINACH LEAVES (OR 50 G/1¾ OZ CRESS AND 50 G/1¾ OZ SPINACH), WASHED AND DRIED

75 G (2¾ OZ) PEAS, THAWED IF FROZEN; IF USING FRESH PEAS BLANCH IN BOILING WATER FOR 2 MINUTES

2 X 200 G (7 OZ) SMOKED CHICKEN BREASTS, THINLY SLICED CROSSWAYS

150 G (5½ OZ) KOHLRABI OR CELERIAC, THINLY SLICED AND LIGHTLY PICKLED (SEE PAGE 34)

2 TABLESPOONS LIGHTLY TOASTED POPPY SEEDS

MUSTARD YOGHURT DRESSING

150 G (5½ OZ) NATURAL YOGHURT

2 TABLESPOONS FINNISH SWEET MUSTARD (PAGE 43) (OR AMERICAN MUSTARD, PLUS A TEASPOON OF HONEY)

Combine the dressing ingredients in a bowl.

Arrange the spinach on serving plates and top with the peas, chicken slices and kohlrabi or celeriac. Scatter over the poppy seeds.

Dollop some of the yoghurt dressing onto the sides of the plates so it can be mixed through the ingredients while eating.

Duck, charred cucumber & malt

This dish typifies new Nordic cuisine, borrowing a traditional technique but applying it to a different ingredient. In this case, cucumber takes on a delightful smokiness reminiscent of eggplant (aubergine) in baba ghanoush. Serve the rich duck with this sweet and earthy malt crumble alongside the crisp acidity of the apple and you will have a well-balanced contemporary dish that isn't too complicated to make.

SERVES 4

1 GRANNY SMITH APPLE, CORED AND THINLY SLICED INTO ACIDULATED WATER

DUCK

2 APPLES, CORED AND HALVED

350 G (12½ OZ) DUCK LEGS (BREASTS CAN BE USED BUT THEY WILL BE A LITTLE DRIER)

½ FENNEL BULB, CUT INTO 8 WEDGES

1 CARROT, ROUGHLY CHOPPED

2 CELERY STALKS, ROUGHLY CHOPPED

250 ML (8½ FL OZ/1 CUP) CHICKEN STOCK

2 TABLESPOONS APPLE CIDER VINEGAR

MALT CRUMBLE

50 G (1¾ OZ) SALTED BUTTER

60 G (2 OZ) ROLLED (PORRIDGE) OATS

1 TABLESPOON MALT

2 TABLESPOONS BUCKWHEAT FLOUR

CHARRED CUCUMBER

1 TELEGRAPH CUCUMBER

2 TABLESPOONS NATURAL YOGHURT

KALE

100 G (3½ OZ) KALE

1 TABLESPOON OLIVE OIL

Preheat the oven to 170°C (340°F). Lay the apples for the duck, cut side down, in a casserole dish. In a hot frying pan, brown the duck legs, skin side down, until they have rendered all their fat and the skin is golden brown. Turn them over and cook for 1 minute before placing on top of the apples in the casserole.

Sauté the fennel, carrot and celery in the duck fat and then pour in the stock and vinegar. Use these to deglaze the pan, scraping up any bits stuck to the base. Pour the contents of the pan over the duck. Cover the casserole with a layer of foil and then top with the lid. Cook in the oven for 1½ hours.

Meanwhile, make the crumble by rubbing together all the ingredients in a bowl. If the mixture is sticking to your hands, add a little more flour. Spread out the crumble on a baking tray and cook in the oven for 10 minutes, or until golden. If the crumble clumps together in large lumps, break it up with wet hands, then return to the oven for 1 minute. Set aside.

To make the charred cucumber, preheat a grill (broiler), barbecue or chargrill pan. Halve the cucumber lengthways and remove and discard the seeds. Cut each length in half crossways to give you 4 batons. Place them skin side towards the heat and cook for 5 minutes on each side, until soft. You don't want them completely charred but you do want some dark colour. Transfer to a food processor, add the yoghurt and some salt and blend briefly, retaining some texture. Set aside.

When the duck is ready, use two forks to pull the meat apart. Return the meat to the cooking juices to keep it warm.

Wash and pat dry the kale, chopping it into smaller pieces if necessary. Heat the oil in a frying pan until very hot, almost smoking, then add the kale and sauté for less than a minute. Drain on paper towel.

Arrange the drained raw apple slices, shredded duck and kale in serving bowls. Dollop around some cucumber purée and drizzle over some of the juices from the casserole (trying to avoid the fatty, oily parts). The fennel, carrot and celery are just for flavour so you can discard these. Top with malt crumble and serve.

Pork, cabbage & cabbage sauce

Cabbage is rife in Nordic countries and chefs are constantly finding new ways to prepare it. Pairing it with pork is a typical Northern European combination of ingredients that pops up everywhere. In this recipe, stewing the cabbage down produces a sweet rich flavour for the sauce. This is perfect hearty, wintry fare.

SERVES 4

2 TABLESPOONS RAPESEED OIL

2 JUNIPER BERRIES, CRUSHED WITH A LITTLE SALT USING A MORTAR AND PESTLE

4 X 200–300 G (7–10½ OZ) PORK STEAKS

50 G (1¾ OZ) TOASTED HAZELNUTS, CHOPPED, TO GARNISH

1 HEIRLOOM BEETROOT (BEET), SLICED VERY THINLY AND QUICKLY PICKLED IN HEAVY PICKLING SOLUTION (SEE PAGE 34), TO GARNISH

CABBAGE SAUCE

1 KG (2 LB 3 OZ) CABBAGE, ½ THINLY SLICED, ½ CUT INTO WEDGES

50 G (1¾ OZ) SMOKED BACON LARDONS OR CHOPPED RASHERS (SLICES)

50 G (1¾ OZ) SALTED BUTTER

250 ML (8½ FL OZ/1 CUP) WHITE WINE

500 ML (17 FL OZ/2 CUPS) CHICKEN STOCK

1 TABLESPOON GOLDEN SYRUP OR TREACLE

100 ML (3½ FL OZ) POURING (SINGLE/LIGHT) CREAM

BEAN PURÉE

100 ML (3½ FL OZ) FULL-CREAM (WHOLE) MILK

450 G (1 LB) TINNED CANNELLINI BEANS

PINCH OF FRESHLY GRATED NUTMEG

1 SMALL GARLIC CLOVE, SLICED

1½ TABLESPOONS CRÈME FRAÎCHE OR SOUR CREAM

In a heavy-based saucepan over a low heat, gently sweat the sliced cabbage and bacon in the butter for just under an hour, until soft and lightly caramelised.

Pour in the wine and stock and simmer for 15 minutes with the lid on.

Reserving the sauce in a bowl, drain the cabbage through a fine sieve. Press the cabbage with the back of a spoon to get out as much liquid as possible. Discard.

Add the golden syrup or treacle to the reserved liquid then pour into a saucepan. Place over a medium heat and cook until the sauce has reduced to one-third of its original volume. Stir in the cream. Season to taste.

To make the bean purée, heat the milk, cannellini beans, nutmeg and garlic in a small saucepan until the milk is steaming. Transfer to a blender, add the crème fraîche or sour cream and blend to a smooth purée. Check the seasoning before returning to the pan.

Preheat the oven to 220°C (430°F). Lightly oil the cabbage wedges with 1 tablespoon of the rapeseed oil. Season, then place on a baking tray lined with baking paper. Roast in the oven for 20 minutes, turning halfway through.

Rub the juniper and salt mix over the pork steaks. Heat the remaining oil in a chargrill pan or frying pan until hot. Fry the steaks for 5–8 minutes on each side until cooked through. Check that they are cooked by slicing into the thickest part of the meat; it should be white all the way through with no pink.

Reheat the cabbage sauce, aerating it with a coffee frother or whisk for a lighter consistency, if you like. Spoon the bean purée on to plates and top with the cabbage wedges and then the pork. Pour over the cabbage sauce before garnishing with the hazelnuts and pickled beetroot.

Roast pork, carrot 'chutney' & sunflower cream

Flæskesteg *(roast pork with crackling) is hugely popular in Denmark. You'll often find it sitting under a heat lamp in smørrebrød eateries. Denmark is actually one of the world's largest producers of pork, exporting as much as 90 per cent to places as far flung as Nepal. A pork production cooperative set up in 1890 resulted in there being three pigs for every human by 1970. That figure has now reached five pigs per person: 25 million animals! This recipe is based on a traditional roast but the vinegar brings a little more acidity to the vegetables, balanced by the nutty cream.*

SERVES 4

800 G (1 LB 12 OZ) SMALL CARROTS

2 ONIONS, UNPEELED

2 GARLIC BULBS

1 TABLESPOON RAPESEED OIL

PINCH OF WHITE PEPPER

800 G (1 LB 12 OZ) PORK LOIN

CHUTNEY

1 LARGE ONION, FINELY DICED

3 CM (1¼ IN) PIECE FRESH GINGER, PEELED AND GRATED

2 TEASPOONS MUSTARD SEEDS

1 TABLESPOON SUNFLOWER OIL

80 ML (2¾ FL OZ/⅓ CUP) APPLE CIDER VINEGAR

SUNFLOWER CREAM

50 G (1¾ OZ) TOASTED SUNFLOWER SEEDS

JUICE OF ½ LEMON

2 TABLESPOONS CHOPPED FLAT-LEAF PARSLEY OR MARJORAM

250 G (9 OZ/1 CUP) CRÈME FRAÎCHE

Preheat the oven to 200°C (400°F). Toss the carrots, whole onions and garlic bulbs in the rapeseed oil and season with salt and a pinch of white pepper.

Place the pork in a large casserole dish or roasting tray and arrange the vegetables around it. Roast in the oven for 40 minutes – 1 hour. To be sure it's ready, use a meat thermometer to check that the internal temperature has reached 70°C (160°F). If you don't have one, insert a skewer into the thickest part of the meat and make sure the juices run clear.

For the chutney, sauté the onion, ginger and mustard seeds in the sunflower oil in a frying pan over a low heat for 3–4 minutes, until soft. Set the pan aside.

When the pork is ready set it aside to rest, peel the roasted onions and garlic and reserve the flesh. Chop the carrots into thirds.

Return the chutney pan to the stove top over a medium heat. Pour in the vinegar and any juices from the roasting tray. Use these to deglaze the onion mixture, scraping up any bits that are stuck to the pan.

Add the reserved garlic and onion flesh and the carrots and toss together for a couple of minutes as you would a stir-fry.

To make the sunflower cream, blitz together all the ingredients with a little salt for 1 minute, until smooth.

Serve slices of the roast pork with the chunky chutney and the sunflower seed cream on the side.

Stout lamb, lentils & cranberry

In keeping with all things grainy and earthy, this book couldn't go without a recipe using stout. The deep barley, malt and coffee characteristics of the beer really get inside the lamb in this stew. Although stews are very traditional in Nordic countries, they usually use cream; this one is a little lighter with a sharper flavour. Baby onions are essential, providing sweetness, along with the simultaneously sweet and tart cranberries. Like most slow-cooks, it is best after it has sat for a while. My suggestion is to double the quantities so you have some for the freezer; it will keep for up to three months.

SERVES 4

2 TABLESPOONS RAPESEED OIL

800 G (1 LB 12 OZ) LEG OR SHOULDER OF LAMB, CUT INTO LARGE DICE

2 TABLESPOONS PLAIN (ALL-PURPOSE) FLOUR

1 TABLESPOON MALT VINEGAR

500 ML (17 FL OZ/2 CUPS) STOUT

1 ONION, FINELY CHOPPED

2 CELERY STALKS, FINELY CHOPPED

2 GARLIC CLOVES, FINELY CHOPPED

2 CLOVES

500 ML (17 FL OZ/2 CUPS) VEGETABLE STOCK

400 G (14 OZ) BABY PEARL ONIONS

100 G (3½ OZ) DRIED CRANBERRIES

200 G (7 OZ) DRIED GREEN OR BROWN LENTILS

1 TABLESPOON CHOPPED DILL

Preheat the oven to 180°C (350°F).

Heat 1 tablespoon of the oil in a large frying pan over a high heat. Brown the lamb for a few minutes on all sides. Season and scatter over the flour. Cook for 1 minute until the flour has soaked up all the liquid. Pour in the vinegar and 1 tablespoon water. Use these to deglaze the pan, scraping up any bits stuck to the base. Transfer the lamb and the juices to a casserole dish and pour over the stout.

Wipe the pan clean, and fry the onion, celery and garlic in the remaining oil for 4–5 minutes, until the vegetables are soft. Add the cloves and deglaze the pan with the stock. Transfer to the casserole. Cover with foil then top with the lid and cook in the oven for 1½ hours. Halfway through cooking, add the pearl onions; in the last 15 minutes add the cranberries.

While the lamb is cooking, thoroughly rinse the lentils under running water. Tip them into a saucepan with ¾ teaspoon salt and pour in 500 ml (17 fl oz/2 cups) water. Bring to the boil over a medium–high heat, then reduce the heat to maintain a gentle simmer. You should only see a few small bubbles and some slight movement in the lentils. Cook, uncovered, for 20–30 minutes, until they are al dente. Add water as needed to make sure the lentils are always just covered. Drain the lentils then stir through the dill. Serve alongside the lamb with a green salad.

Beef brisket, spiced wine & cauliflower steaks

Warm mulled wine on a snowy day is a simple pleasure that no Nordic country misses out on around Christmas time, but this recipe finds another great use for it. The deep, developed flavour from the spices makes for a simple ready-to-go marinade and the sugar acts as a brine, lightly penetrating the meat before cooking, helping to tenderise it. So you don't burn the sugar when sealing the meat, I suggest using a lower temperature than you would normally.

SERVES 4

250 ML (8½ FL OZ/1 CUP) MULLED WINE, SPICED WINE OR GLOGG

25 G (1 OZ) THYME, LEAVES PICKED

1.5 KG (3 LB 5 OZ) BEEF BRISKET (OX CHEEK CAN ALSO BE USED)

2 TABLESPOONS RAPESEED OIL

3 LARGE ONIONS, PEELED

600 G (1 LB 5 OZ) CAULIFLOWER

1 TABLESPOON SALTED BUTTER

Place the wine, thyme and beef in a sealed bag. Rub the wine and thyme into the meat then leave in the refrigerator overnight.

When you're ready to cook the beef, preheat the oven to 170°C (340°F). Heat 1 tablespoon of the oil in a frying pan over a medium heat and seal the beef on all sides. You want it to take on quite a dark colour.

Halve the onions and lay them in the bottom of a roasting tray. Place the brisket on top, fat side up, and pour over the marinade. Cover with a layer of baking paper then seal the roasting tray with a double thickness of foil to help keep in the moisture. Roast in the oven for 3–3½ hours. Check on it after 2 hours and if it has dried out, add 300 ml (10 fl oz) of water.

Remove and discard the outer leaves from the cauliflower. Reserve a few florets and lightly pickle them following the instructions on page 43.

Steam the remaining whole cauliflower for 5–8 minutes. Alternatively, bring to a boil in a large pot of salted water and, once boiling, simmer for 5 minutes. Gently place the cooked cauliflower somewhere to cool and dry. Once it has cooled carefully slice it vertically into 2–3 cm (¾–1¼ in) thick steaks. Some will crumble but most should hold their shape. Season well.

When the beef is cooked, remove from the roasting tray and place on a board or plate. Cover in foil and leave to rest while you make a sauce.

Pour the liquid from the roasting tray into a jug. Separate and discard the fat by using a gravy skimmer or by placing ice cubes quickly into the liquid to attract the fat, then throw them away. Pour the juices into a saucepan and reduce over a medium heat to a sauce consistency.

In a large frying pan, fry the cauliflower steaks in the butter and the remaining oil for a few minutes on each side, until golden.

Serve chunks of beef on top of the cauliflower steaks. Pour over the sauce and garnish with the lightly pickled thin slices of cauliflower florets.

CHAPTER SIX

From the Forest

My first encounter with Scandinavian forests came from seeing Norsca commercials and tourist brochures in the eighties. They got it right: endless birch and pine trees, moss-covered rocks and streams – although perhaps a few too many ferns. What people might not have learned from the adverts, however, is that there is a diverse range of edibles that the forest delivers.

The principal fruits found in the forest are lingonberries and blueberries, but there are plenty more besides: white-, red-, and blackcurrants, raspberries, wild strawberries, blackberries, rowanberries, elderberries . . . the Arctic plains even offer up cloudberries, which can only be found this far north. And these fruits never taste better than they do in that moment, standing in the dappled shadows of thousands of trees, picked fresh and straight on to the taste buds. A harmony of sweet and sour. Back in the kitchen, these perfect fruits often need nothing more than a splash of milk or a lick of cream. Or they can be turned into marmalades, jams, liqueurs and fruit syrups to be stored away and savoured during the cold season. Nearby, you will find an abundance of wild greens: sorrel, ramsons, nettle, angelica and woodruff, to name a few.

Yet, the forest yields much more than what you can find growing on the ground, in trees and on bushes. With thousands of kilometres of almost uninterrupted birch and pine, the woods of Norway, Sweden and Finland in particular contain a great deal of interest for the hunter. Roebuck, elk (or moose), reindeer, red deer, fallow deer, wild boar, beaver, as well as an array of birds present a whole new challenge for those wishing to source their own food. This chapter uses ingredients sourced from the forest but that are readily available outside of the Nordic region.

Ramsons paste toastie

It's the freshness of flavour in this forest herb that makes it so special. Known interchangeably as ramsons, wood garlic and wild garlic, it lives up to its name, tasting mostly garlicky, but also with a kick of spring onion (scallion). It's a very versatile ingredient: line pork belly with it before rolling, use it to stuff chicken or toss it through any number of dishes in the final stages of cooking. Seek it out if you can.

MAKES 4

75 G (2¾ OZ) SALTED BUTTER

8 THICK SLICES OF SOURDOUGH BREAD

200 G (7 OZ) MILD CHEESE, SUCH AS GOUDA OR EDAM, SLICED

RAMSONS PASTE

100 G (3½ OZ) WILD GARLIC, RINSED AND DRAINED

50 G (1¾ OZ) VASTERBOTTEN CHEESE (OR PARMESAN), ROUGHLY CHOPPED

50 G (1¾ OZ/⅓ CUP) WHOLE ALMONDS

1 TEASPOON SEA SALT

PINCH OF WHITE PEPPER

75 ML (2½ FL OZ) RAPESEED OIL

Combine all the paste ingredients except for the oil in a blender. Scrape down the sides, then turn on the blender again and slowly add the oil. Keep the motor running until the mixture is fully combined; you may need to stop and scrape down the sides again. Check the seasoning: depending on the type of cheese you use, it may need more salt. It can now be transferred to a sterilised jar and kept in the refrigerator for up to 5 days. (To sterilise a glass jar, wash it thoroughly in hot soapy water, rinse well, then put it on a baking tray in a low oven (120°C/250°F) for 20 minutes. Leave to cool.)

To make the toasties, butter one side of each slice of sourdough and slather ramsons paste on the other side of 4 of them. Top the paste with slices of cheese and sandwich the bread together, butter sides out.

In batches, depending on the size of your frying pan, fry the sandwiches over a low heat for 3–4 minutes, until golden brown underneath, then flip them over and cook for 3–4 minutes on the other side. Use a spatula to press down on the toasties or a heavy plate to weigh them down. Serve with a salad.

Chanterelles, buckwheat crepes & kale

In the autumn, golden chanterelle mushrooms are such a prized find in Nordic forests that they often overshadow the huge array of other fungi on offer. But I think rightly so: their sweet, nutty flavour is unique and delicious. Eating them simply fried in butter and parsley and piled on toast is a joy in itself. For weeks of the year they pop up in the shadows of logs on the forest floor, at times in huge abundance. Many Nordic folk have secret spots they return to, to harvest them. If you are in luck, pick as many as you can manage and fry them in butter and freeze any you aren't going to eat at once; they will keep very well frozen for up to six months. In this recipe, the buckwheat crepes and kale enhance their earthiness, while the salty sharp goat's cheese lifts all the flavours.

SERVES 4

SALTED BUTTER, FOR FRYING

BATTER

60 ML (2 FL OZ/¼ CUP) VEGETABLE OIL, PLUS EXTRA FOR FRYING

190 ML (6½ FL OZ/¾ CUP) FULL-CREAM (WHOLE) MILK

3 LARGE EGGS

310 G (11 OZ) BUCKWHEAT FLOUR

FILLING

100 G (3½ OZ) KALE, ROUGHLY CHOPPED

1 TABLESPOON SALTED BUTTER

½ TABLESPOON RAPESEED OIL

300 G (10½ OZ) CHANTERELLE MUSHROOMS, BRUSHED CLEAN, THE LARGER ONES TORN IN HALF

150 G (5½ OZ) CREAMY FETA OR GOAT'S CHEESE

First make the batter. Whisk the vegetable oil, milk, 310 ml (10½ fl oz/ 1¼ cups) water and the eggs together vigorously in a large bowl. Gradually add the flour and a pinch of salt, whisking all the time, until well incorporated. Chill in the refrigerator for 30 minutes.

While the batter is resting, make a start on the filling. Put the chopped kale in a bowl and pour over a kettle of boiling water. Leave for 3–4 minutes, then drain and pat dry.

To cook the crepes, heat a little butter in a frying pan. When it is foaming, pour in enough batter to create a thin layer on the base of the pan. Lift, tilt and rotate the pan so that the batter forms an even, very thin layer. Cook for 30 seconds–1 minute, until bubbles start to appear on the surface and the edges are solid and easy to lift up with a spatula. Flip over and continue cooking for the same amount of time. Stack the cooked crepes on a plate covered with a clean dry tea towel (dish towel), while you cook the rest. Keep covered while you finish the filling.

Heat the butter and rapeseed oil for the filling in a large frying pan. Add the kale and mushrooms and season. Sauté for a few minutes, until the kale just starts to wilt and the mushrooms are starting to soften.

To serve, crumble some cheese over each crepe. Top with some of the kale and mushrooms, fold and serve.

Chanterelle mushroom mash

The flavour of these mushrooms mixed in with the mashed potatoes is simply a delight. In one kitchen I used to work in, we would serve this rolled up in soft tunnbröd (see page 224), which was then pan-fried. It is also great served with meat. A rather unfamiliar pairing that is common throughout Nordic countries – and one I have been forced to come to terms with – is mushrooms and fish. Try it for yourself.

SERVES 6

1 KG (2 LB 3 OZ) STARCHY POTATOES, PEELED

200 G (7 OZ) CHANTERELLE MUSHROOMS, BRUSHED CLEAN, THE LARGER ONES TORN IN HALF

2 TEASPOONS CHOPPED THYME

1 TABLESPOON RAPESEED OIL

25 G (1 OZ) SALTED BUTTER

WHITE PEPPER

300 ML (10 FL OZ) FULL-CREAM (WHOLE) MILK

Boil the potatoes in a large saucepan of salted water for 12–15 minutes, or until soft.

Meanwhile, sauté the mushrooms and thyme in the oil and half the butter in a frying pan over a medium heat. Season well with salt and white pepper. Once the mushrooms have softened and released some of their liquid, remove the pan from the heat and set aside.

Put the milk and the remaining butter in a small saucepan. Season, then gently warm over low heat until the milk is steaming. Do not let it boil.

Drain the potatoes well and return them to the hot pan to help them dry out. For best results, put the potatoes through a ricer, alternatively, use a masher. Mix the buttery milk mixture into the potatoes using a wooden spoon until it forms a smooth purée. Stir through the mushrooms, check the seasoning and serve.

Nettle dumplings, rhubarb & bacon

If you have any difficulty visually identifying nettles then you can always use the touch method; I can assure you any doubt will be swiftly removed. Pick them in the spring when they grow abundantly in woods and, perhaps surprisingly, in urban green areas. Once they have flowered, you are sadly too late. If you are having trouble finding a stash, check near any blackberry bushes you know of: they usually compete for territory. They are incredibly healthy and it can be a fun forage, getting all geared up to avoid the sting.

SERVES 4

200 G (7 OZ) THIN SMOKED BACON RASHERS (SLICES)

1 TABLESPOON RAPESEED OIL

½ QUANTITY RHUBARB CHUTNEY (PAGE 49), TO SERVE

PEA TENDRILS, TO GARNISH (OPTIONAL)

NETTLE DUMPLINGS

200 G (7 OZ) NETTLES (AROUND HALF A SHOPPING BAG IF FRESHLY PICKED)

1 TABLESPOON RAPESEED OIL

PINCH OF WHITE PEPPER

3 EGG YOLKS

200 G (7 OZ) FRESH RICOTTA

ABOUT 60 G (2 OZ) PLAIN (ALL-PURPOSE) FLOUR

Wearing gloves, wash the nettles several times under running water. Use your hands to remove some of the fuzz from the leaves and stems. Chop them roughly then fry them in the oil in a frying pan over a medium heat until they wilt like spinach. Season to taste with salt and white pepper, then tip on to a plate and allow to cool.

In a food processor, or with a whisk in a large bowl, combine the egg yolks, nettles and ricotta. Add as little flour as you need just to form a light dough. Taste and check the seasoning.

To form the dumplings, roll a teaspoon of dough between your palms into a little oval shape, or use two spoons to make a quenelle. Place on a sheet of baking paper and repeat with the remaining dough. Cover with a damp clean tea towel (dish towel).

Preheat the oven to 90°C (195°F). Bring 2 litres (68 fl oz/8 cups) salted water to a simmer in a large saucepan. Carefully drop in batches of the dumplings, about 5 at a time. Cook for 2 minutes, or until they float to the top. Transfer to a baking tray and keep warm in the oven while you cook the rest.

Meanwhile, fry the bacon in the oil in a frying pan over a medium–high heat to desired doneness. Serve with the dumplings, relish and pea tendrils (if using).

Venison, grilled plums & celery

Traditionally, venison is served as a smoked cold cut, cooked rare, stewed (popular in Norway) or else it is prepared as by the Sami culture from northern Sweden, where it is shaved and heavily salted, resembling kebab meat. It has a gamey quality that can be likened to other lean wild meats like kangaroo and horse, and it pairs well with sweeter elements in dishes – in Sweden it is almost always served with lingonberry jam. Using this as inspiration, in this recipe I have paired it with grilled plums.

SERVES 4

50 G (1¾ OZ/⅓ CUP) RAW ALMONDS

200 G (7 OZ) WHEATBERRY (ALSO KNOWN AS WHEAT KERNEL; CRACKED WHEAT CAN BE SUBSTITUTED)

1 CELERY HEART, LEAVES AND ALL

2 DRIED JUNIPER BERRIES

2 TEASPOONS SEA SALT FLAKES

800 G (1 LB 12 OZ) VENISON FILLET

1 TABLESPOON RAPESEED OIL

4 RED PLUMS, HALVED AND PITTED

2 TABLESPOONS NATURAL YOGHURT

PINCH OF WHITE PEPPER

1 TEASPOON MAPLE SYRUP

Put the almonds in a bowl and cover with water so that they are fully submerged.

Meanwhile, boil 250 ml (8½ fl oz/1 cup) salted water in a saucepan, then add the wheatberry. Reduce the heat and simmer with the lid on for 15 minutes, until the grains have absorbed all the water. Set aside, with the lid still on.

Using a mandoline if you have one, thinly slice the inner stalks of the celery lengthways into a bowl of cold water. Reserve any leaves and the outer stalks for the sauce. Preheat the oven to 180°C (350°F).

Using a mortar and pestle grind the juniper berries with the salt and use the mixture to season the venison on all sides.

Heat the oil in an ovenproof frying pan over a high heat and fry the venison for 30 seconds on each side to seal the meat. Transfer to the oven to cook through. How long it needs will depend on the thickness of the meat and how well it was sealed in the pan; 15–20 minutes is usually enough. You want the meat to be quite rare so it should just spring back when you press it. Remove from the oven and place on a board. Cover with foil and leave to rest in a warm place for 10 minutes. Preheat the grill (broiler) (or a barbecue) to a high heat.

While the venison is resting, grill the plums for 3 minutes on each side, until lightly charred, then set aside.

Drain the almonds, then, using a mandoline, carefully shave into small, thin slices.

Blitz any left-over celery leaves and stems in a blender with the yoghurt, a pinch of white pepper, the maple syrup and any resting juices from the venison. If the consistency is a little thick, add some water. Taste and check the seasoning.

Thinly slice the venison. Cut the plums into quarters. Arrange the drained celery, wheat, plums and venison on a large platter, garnish with the almond shavings and drizzle over the yoghurt sauce.

Venison, pickled chanterelles & mustard rye crumble

Venison, like all game, is a very lean meat. It goes well with bitter and sweet flavours, and in many traditional Nordic recipes it's cooked as a stew with cream. I love it cured or served rare and cold as it is here. Left-over venison can be added to salads or served on crispbread.

It's best to prepare these pickled chanterelles at least a day in advance, so that the mushrooms can settle in the pickling solution.

SERVES 2 WITH LEFTOVERS

100 G (3½ OZ) CHANTERELLES, CLEANED WITH A BRUSH AND LARGER MUSHROOMS TORN IN HALF

300 G (10½ OZ) SMALL NEW POTATOES

15 G (½ OZ) SALTED BUTTER

3 TARRAGON SPRIGS, LEAVES PICKED, PLUS EXTRA TO GARNISH

1 X 400 G (14 OZ) VENISON FILLET

1 TABLESPOON RAPESEED OIL

ROSEHIP KETCHUP (OR ANY RELISH OR CHUTNEY) TO SERVE

LIGHT PICKLING SOLUTION

300 ML (10 FL OZ) APPLE-CIDER VINEGAR

150 G (5½ OZ) CASTER (SUPERFINE) SUGAR

1 TEASPOON SALT

3 DRIED JUNIPER BERRIES

2 ALLSPICE BERRIES

2 BAY LEAVES

MUSTARD RYE CRUMBLE

125 G (4½ OZ/1 CUP) RYE FLAKES

2 TABLESPOONS RAPESEED OIL

1 TEASPOON DIJON MUSTARD

1 TEASPOON HONEY

For the pickling solution, put all the ingredients in a saucepan along with 200 ml (7 fl oz) of cold water. Bring to a boil then reduce the heat and simmer gently, stirring, for 2 minutes, until all the sugar has dissolved. Remove from the heat and set aside to cool.

Place the chanterelles in a non-reactive bowl and pour over the cooled pickling liquid. Leave for at least 30 minutes, preferably overnight.

When ready to cook, add the potatoes to a saucepan of boiling water and cook them until they are tender and easily pierced with the point of a knife. Drain, add the butter and tarragon and toss together. Keep warm with the lid on.

Preheat the oven to 180°C (350°F). Line a baking tray with baking paper.

To make the mustard rye crumble, combine all the ingredients in a bowl. Arrange spoonfuls of the mixture on the prepared baking tray and bake for 5–8 minutes, until golden brown. Remove from the oven and leave to cool and crisp up.

Season the venison fillet well with sea salt and freshly ground black pepper. Heat the oil in an ovenproof frying pan or cast-iron grill pan over a high heat, add the venison and fry for 30 seconds on each side to seal the meat. Transfer to the oven to cook through. How long it needs will depend on the thickness of the meat and how well it was sealed in the pan; 8–10 minutes is usually enough. You want the meat to be quite rare so it should just spring back when you press it. Remove from the oven and place on a board. Cover with foil and leave to rest in a warm place for 10 minutes.

To serve, cut the rested venison fillet into very thin slices and divide between serving plates. Top with the mustard rye crumble, pickled mushrooms and tarragon sprigs and serve with the potatoes and rosehip ketchup, but any relish or chutney would substitute well.

Pine, pancakes & pollen

I'm not suggesting you eat your Christmas tree but pine needles have a minty, fresh flavour that is perfect for infusing broths, soups and syrups, or creams and custards as shown here. Not all pine is edible. Some trees, such as the Australian pine (she-oak) and some varieties of casuarinas look like they have pine needles but they are actually not pine trees at all. Fir and spruce are the best options. Harvest tender new-growth tips when they first emerge from their brown papery casings. This recipe tells you how to make one large stack of pancakes to cut into wedges. You can also make stacks of mini pancakes, as shown in the photograph.

SERVES 4–6

150 G (5½ OZ/1 CUP) PLAIN (ALL-PURPOSE) FLOUR

250 ML (8½ FL OZ/1 CUP) FULL-CREAM (WHOLE) MILK

125 ML (4 FL OZ/½ CUP) LUKEWARM WATER OR LAGER

3 TABLESPOONS CASTER (SUPERFINE) SUGAR

4 LARGE EGGS

80 G (2¾ OZ) UNSALTED BUTTER, MELTED

50 G (1¾ OZ) DRIED POLLEN, TO GARNISH

RUNNY HONEY, TO SERVE

PINE CUSTARD

500 ML (17 FL OZ/2 CUPS) FULL-CREAM (WHOLE) MILK

2 X 10–15 CM (4–6 IN) SPRUCE PINE BRANCHES, TIPS OR NEEDLES PICKED, OR 2 PINE TEABAGS

6 LARGE EGG YOLKS

110 G (4 OZ/½ CUP) CASTER (SUPERFINE) SUGAR

30 G (1 OZ) CORNFLOUR (CORNSTARCH)

2 TABLESPOONS UNSALTED BUTTER, AT ROOM TEMPERATURE

150 ML (5½ FL OZ) WHIPPING CREAM, WHIPPED (OPTIONAL)

First make the custard. Heat the milk in a small saucepan until it is just steaming; do not let it simmer. If you have a kitchen thermometer it should be 60–80°C (140–175°F). Add the pine tips or needles or the pine teabags and infuse for 10 minutes. Taste, and if you can detect the pine flavour, strain the milk into a jug. If you'd like a stronger flavour, leave for a few more minutes.

Whisk together the yolks, sugar and cornflour in a bowl. Stir in one-quarter of the infused milk and whisk vigorously. Pour in the rest of the milk and whisk until smooth. Return the custard to the pan and bring to the boil over a medium heat, whisking vigorously. Cook for 1–2 minutes, still whisking, until the mixture thickens. Set the base of the pan in an ice-cold water bath or place in the freezer to cool, stirring frequently so that the mixture remains smooth. When it is almost cool, stir in the butter, then chill in the refrigerator.

While the custard is cooling, make the pancake batter. In a bowl or using a food processor, combine the flour, milk, water or lager, sugar, eggs, half the butter and a pinch of salt; it should have a thick but pourable consistency. Cover the bowl with plastic wrap and refrigerate for at least 1 hour.

When you're ready to cook the pancakes, place a non-stick frying pan over a medium heat. Using paper towel, coat the pan with the remaining butter. Pour 2–3 tablespoons of batter into the pan. Lift, tilt and rotate the pan so that the batter forms an even, very thin layer. Cook for 30 seconds–1 minute, until golden underneath then flip over the pancake and cook for the same amount of time. Stack the cooked pancakes on a plate and cover with plastic wrap or a slightly damp clean tea towel (dish towel), while you cook the rest. Leave to cool.

Whiz the custard in a food processor for 10 seconds. If you would like a lighter, airier custard, fold in some whipped cream. Layer the cooled pancakes with the custard, reserving some to spread on top. Cover with plastic wrap and chill in the refrigerator for at least 1 hour. When ready to serve, spread the remaining custard over the top. Sprinkle with the pollen, drizzle over some honey and cut into wedges.

Elderflower sherbet ice & buttermilk sponge

The surprisingly floral, sweet intensity of this elderflower ice provides a great contrast to the sourness in the cake. Serve it immediately to avoid the cake getting soggy from the melting ice.

SERVES 4

ELDERFLOWER SHERBET ICE

150 ML (5 FL OZ) ELDERFLOWER CORDIAL (SEE PAGE 62)

500 ML (17 FL OZ/2 CUPS) FRESH APPLE PURÉE (AROUND 4 APPLES, PEELED, CORED AND BLENDED)

1 EGG WHITE

ELDERFLOWERS, TO GARNISH (OPTIONAL)

BUTTERMILK SPONGE

125 G (4½ OZ) UNSALTED BUTTER, SOFTENED, PLUS EXTRA FOR GREASING

220 G (8 OZ) PLAIN (ALL-PURPOSE) FLOUR

70 G (2½ OZ) CASTER (SUPERFINE) SUGAR

70 G (2½ OZ) SOFT LIGHT BROWN SUGAR

2 LARGE EGGS

2 TABLESPOONS HONEY

1 TEASPOON BAKING POWDER

½ TEASPOON MIXED SPICE

2 TABLESPOONS BUTTERMILK

To make the elderflower sherbet ice, whisk together all the ingredients along with 150 ml (5 fl oz) water in a bowl and then pour into a ceramic dish or baking tray. Freeze overnight.

Heat the oven to 160°C (320°F). Grease and line a 25 cm (10 in) round cake tin with baking paper.

Put all the sponge ingredients into a large bowl with a pinch of salt and beat using an electric mixer for about 5 minutes, until smooth.

Pour the batter into the prepared tin and bake for about 25 minutes, until a skewer inserted into the middle of the cake comes out clean. Turn out on to a wire rack to cool.

About 20 minutes before serving, remove the sherbet ice from the freezer and leave at room temperature for 5–10 minutes, depending on how warm your kitchen is. Scrape half the depth with a fork to create 'snow'. Return to the freezer for 10 minutes. Remove and scrape some more. Tear chunks from the cake, place in bowls and top with the sherbet ice and the elderflowers (if using).

Rosehip syrup, baked yoghurt & cardamom crumble

In Sweden, warm rosehip soup is an iconic dish. It even comes in powdered form to which you just add hot water. I, however, prefer rosehip syrup to soup. It is a sweet concentration of all those zesty but floral flavours. All the flavour is in the skin of the rosehip – the middle being full of lots of annoying seeds, hence the excessive straining in this recipe. But it is worth the effort. Rosehips are best picked from wild rose bushes in autumn, when they are ripe and deep in colour.

SERVES 4

500 G (1 LB 2 OZ/2 CUPS) NATURAL YOGHURT

200 ML (7 FL OZ) SWEETENED CONDENSED MILK (I USED CARAMELISED CONDENSED MILK, ALSO KNOWN AS DULCE DE LECHE)

ROSEHIP SYRUP

1 KG (2 LB 3 OZ) ROSEHIPS, TRIMMED OF ALL LEAVES AND WASHED

UP TO 500 G (1 LB 2 OZ) CASTER (SUPERFINE) SUGAR

CRUMBLE

60 G (2 OZ) PLAIN (ALL-PURPOSE) FLOUR

1 TEASPOON GROUND CARDAMOM

1 TABLESPOON MUSCOVADO SUGAR

40 G (1½ OZ) UNSALTED BUTTER, AT ROOM TEMPERATURE

If you aren't going to use all the syrup at once, sterilise a couple of glass bottles or jars. Wash them thoroughly in hot soapy water, rinse well, then put them on a tray in a low oven (120°C/250°F) for 20 minutes. Leave to cool.

Use a food processor to roughly chop batches of the rosehips. Transfer to a large saucepan. Add 1.25 litres (42 fl oz/5 cups) water and bring to the boil over a high heat. Reduce the heat and simmer for 15 minutes.

Strain the rosehips through a double layer of muslin (cheesecloth) into a bowl, letting it sit for at least 30 minutes. Cut out a fresh piece of muslin. Fold it over to double the thickness and then pass the strained juice through once more.

Measure the rosehip juice into a large clean saucepan and for every 500 ml (17 fl oz/2 cups) add 325 g (11½ oz) sugar. Heat gently, stirring, until the sugar has dissolved, then increase the heat and bring to the boil. Boil for 3 minutes, skimming off any scum on the surface. At this point the syrup can be decanted into the prepared bottles and sealed. It will keep in the refrigerator for a few months. To make this dessert you will need to reduce the syrup for a few minutes in a saucepan set over a medium heat, until it has the consistency of maple syrup.

Preheat the oven to 150°C (300°F). Mix the yoghurt and condensed milk in a bowl until smooth. Pour into a shallow ovenproof dish, about 20 cm (8 in) wide and 5 cm (2 in) deep, or four 200 ml (7 fl oz) ramekins. Bake the yoghurt for 30 minutes for a larger dish or 20 minutes for individual dishes, or until set.

While the yoghurt is baking, combine the flour, cardamom and sugar in a bowl. Use your fingertips to rub in the butter until the mixture has the consistency of loose chunky soil. Spread out on to a baking tray lined with baking paper. Bake for 10–15 minutes until golden brown. Remove from the oven and leave to cool.

When the yoghurt is cooked, cover with plastic wrap and refrigerate until cold (about 1 hour). To serve, pour off any liquid on top of the yoghurts, drizzle over some of the rosehip syrup and sprinkle with the crumble. Any left-over syrup can be used to flavour smoothies or to top ice cream or fresh yoghurt.

Matcha, quinoa & blueberry sails

Seeds and grains play an important role in the new Nordic cooking ideology and the range that can be found in the supermarkets of Nordic countries is very impressive. Puffing grains is tricky to do at home, so here you need to buy the quinoa prepared. Other puffed grains such as amaranth and millet can be used in place of the quinoa – just be sure to measure out the same volume as opposed to weight.

MAKES AT LEAST 12 SAILS

160 G (5¾ OZ/2 CUPS) ROLLED (PORRIDGE) OATS

175G (6 OZ/1 CUP) PEPITAS (PUMPKIN SEEDS)

100 ML (3½ FL OZ) GRAPE SYRUP

3 TABLESPOONS HONEY

1½ TABLESPOONS MATCHA GREEN TEA POWDER (OR TO YOUR TASTE)

3 TABLESPOONS COCONUT OIL

1 TEASPOON NATURAL VANILLA EXTRACT

40 G (1½ OZ/1½ CUPS) UNSWEETENED PUFFED QUINOA GRAINS

155 G (5½ OZ/1 CUP) FRESH BLUEBERRIES

Preheat the oven to 160°C (325°F). Line a 20 cm x 15 cm (8 in x 6 in) baking tin with baking paper.

Arrange the oats and pepitas on a baking tray in an even layer and bake for 10–15 minutes, or until the oats are golden and have a nutty aroma and the pepitas are toasted. Set aside to cool completely.

In a small saucepan over a low heat, stir together the grape syrup, honey, matcha powder, coconut oil and vanilla extract until the coconut oil has melted and the ingredients are well combined.

Pour the syrup mixture into a large bowl. Add the cooled oats, puffed quinoa grains and pepitas to the bowl and quickly stir together to coat them in the liquid, then gently stir through the blueberries. Pour the mixture into the lined tin, pressing firmly into the corners, and transfer to the refrigerator for 1–2 hours to chill and firm up.

To serve, lift the chilled mixture from the baking tin and cut into six squares, then cut the squares diagonally into 12 triangles. These sails will keep well in the refrigerator in a sealed container for up to 2 weeks.

CHAPTER SEVEN

Baking

To generalise that Nordic folk have a sweet tooth wouldn't be wrong. Across the region, whether pre- or post-lunch, it is common to see people taking a quick break from work or holding a meeting over a cup of filter coffee with an accompanying taste of something sweet. So popular is this culture of coffee and cake in Sweden that it even has its own name, *fika*!

Spices are prominent in doughs and batters and there are many varieties of flour, producing a huge range of textures in breads, pastries and cakes. All those warming flavours we know and love – nutmeg, cloves, cinnamon and cardamom – are as likely to cosy up in a mug of mulled wine as they are to find themselves in sweet bakes.

But it is the impressive selection of breads that really deserves our full attention. A good piece of dark rye with butter and a slice of sharp cheese is Sweden's most celebrated chef, Mathias Dahlgren's preferred last meal – with black coffee, of course. Whether crumbled up into *ymer* (page 53), served simply with butter during a meal, or providing the base for the famous *smørrebrød* (see pages 72–5), *ragbröd* is loved all over the region.

Today, traditional breads and crispbreads sit alongside some unusual varieties of softer, sweeter breads: carrot bread, sunflower seed bread and lingonberry bread, to name a few. With such a range of grains and flours to choose from, Nordic chefs have been encouraged to develop some wonderful new recipes for quick-bake breads. The chapter ahead explores some of the classic recipes that you will find all across the region, along with a few more contemporary bakes.

Knäckerbröd

These staple breads are presented at the table during every significant Swedish meal. The top surface is always more undulated than the base and is called the 'rich man's side' because, when you spread it, it gathers more butter in the nooks and crannies. One of knäckerbröd's *best friends is pickled herring along with sliced egg, fish roe from a tube and cucumber, or simply with butter and a good sharp cheese.*

MAKES 6

20 G (¾ OZ) FRESH YEAST

2½ TABLESPOONS GOLDEN SYRUP OR TREACLE

270 ML (9 FL OZ) COLD WATER

400 G (14 OZ/2⅔ CUPS) PLAIN (ALL-PURPOSE) FLOUR

120 G (4½ OZ) COARSE WHOLEGRAIN RYE FLOUR, PLUS EXTRA FOR DUSTING

1 TEASPOON DRIED DILL (OPTIONAL)

1 TEASPOON SALT

100 G (3½ OZ) SUNFLOWER SEEDS

Crumble the yeast into a large bowl and mix with the golden syrup or treacle and water. Add the remaining ingredients, apart from the sunflower seeds, with 1 teaspoon salt and bring together into a dough. Knead the dough for 2 minutes then cover the bowl in a clean tea towel (dish towel) and let it sit at room temperature for 40 minutes.

Preheat the oven to 200°C (400°F). Divide the dough into 6 even-sized amounts and roll each one into a ball. Dust with some extra rye flour, then roll out each ball as thinly as possible. They should be at least 20 cm (8 in) in diameter, but be careful not to tear the dough. Stretching the dough a little like how you would for pizza dough helped me to get them a little thinner.

Roll on a sprinkle of sunflower seeds so they embed themselves in the dough. Traditionally, notched rolling pins (see page 16) are then used to texture the surface of the breads, but these are hard to come by so if you don't have one, use the back of a fork instead.

Use a small glass or cookie cutter (no more than 5 cm/2 in) to cut a hole from the middle. This helps to cook the bread evenly all over. Bake the cuttings too: you can snack on these.

Place the breads on baking trays lined with baking paper and cook in the oven for 5 minutes. If you own perforated baking trays this will help get them lovely and crisp, as they will stop any moisture building up under the breads. When the thinner areas have developed some lovely golden colours, they are ready.

Remove from the oven and hang on string or hooks to cool. Depending on how indulgent you are feeling, serve with butter on the side and the topping of your choice!

Tunnbröd

These 'thin breads' vary enormously. They can be soft or crisp, and can be made from any combination of wheat, barley and rye. Even the rolling pin used to make them can alter their appearance and texture. Also known as Arctic breads, they share a history with crispbreads (see page 227), originating from the northern Nordic regions. So far up in this cold climate, wheat is hard to grow, and only low-gluten grains can flourish: it simply isn't possible to make breads that can rise.

Soft tunnbröd, *as described in this recipe, is commonly used to wrap up fillings – as you might a tortilla. In the photograph, I have used it to wrap up a mixture of gravlax, pickled cucumber, lettuce and crème fraiche. Crisp* tunnbröd *differs from the more common crispbread in being thinner, more compact and containing fewer air bubbles. However, it is served the same way: with almost all meals, simply spread with butter. Traditionally, though,* tunnbröd *is eaten with* surströmming, *a fermented herring, which is something of a national dish in Sweden. It is not given much mention in this book for two reasons: it's hard to find outside the Nordics and the smell you experience on opening a tin.*

MAKES 16

500 ML (17 FL OZ/2 CUPS) FULL-CREAM (WHOLE) MILK

¼ CUP UNSALTED BUTTER, MELTED

2 TEASPOONS DRIED INSTANT YEAST

2 TABLESPOONS HONEY

1 TEASPOON FENNEL SEEDS, CRUSHED USING A MORTAR AND PESTLE

55 G (2 OZ/¼ CUP) CASTER (SUPERFINE) SUGAR

1 TEASPOON SALT

90 G (6½ OZ/¾ CUP) WHOLEGRAIN RYE FLOUR

125 G (4½ OZ/½ CUP) GRAHAM FLOUR (SEE PAGE 296)

450 G (1 LB/3 CUPS) PLAIN (ALL-PURPOSE) FLOUR, PLUS EXTRA FOR DUSTING

½ TEASPOON BICARBONATE OF SODA (BAKING SODA)

Warm the milk and butter in a small saucepan just until it starts to steam. Do not let it simmer. If you have a kitchen thermometer, it should be about 80°C (175°F).

Combine the warm milk and butter mixture, yeast, honey, fennel seeds, sugar and salt in a bowl. Mix well and set aside for a couple of minutes.

Alternate adding small amounts of the flours and bicarbonate of soda, mixing slowly to form a dough. If the dough is a little wet, add a little more plain flour; it should just come away from the side of the bowl without sticking.

Knead until smooth and elastic, then cover with a clean tea towel (dish towel) and leave to rise at room temperature for 45 minutes.

Divide the dough into 16 even-sized amounts and roll into balls. Dust your work surface with flour and then roll out each ball as thinly as possible without tearing the dough. They should be about 10–15 cm (4–6 in) wide. Prick one side of each all over with a fork.

Heat a dry non-stick frying pan to over a medium-high heat and cook the breads one at a time for a minute on each side; they should 'freckle' with small brown dots. If the bread is crunchy, then you have cooked it for too long so cook the next one for a little less time. Stack the cooked discs underneath a clean slightly damp tea towel so that they can steam and not dry out. Once cooled, they should resemble soft tortillas.

Seedy crispbreads

Seeds and grains play a big part in new Nordic cooking. The climate isn't well suited to growing wheat, so hardier grains such as oats, barley and rye – as well as seeds – are more popular. This recipe is quick to make, simple and delicious. Top the bread with prawn rora *(see page 79), slices of smoked salmon or simply smear with butter and sprinkle over a little flaked salt. Beware: they are very moreish.*

MAKES 8–10

120 G (4½ OZ) PLAIN (ALL-PURPOSE) FLOUR

60 G (2 OZ) LINSEEDS (FLAX SEEDS)

70 G (2½ OZ) SESAME SEEDS

60 G (2 OZ/½ CUP) SUNFLOWER SEEDS

200 ML (7 FL OZ) COLD WATER

½ TEASPOON SALT

½–1 TEASPOON TOASTED AND GROUND FENNEL SEEDS (OPTIONAL)

1 TEASPOON SEA SALT FLAKES

Preheat the oven to 170°C (340°F). In a bowl, mix together all the ingredients apart from the sea salt flakes.

Using a spatula, spread the mixture over a sheet of baking paper. The aim is for it to be as thin as possible, without producing any holes. It can help to sprinkle a little flour over the mixture, then lay a second sheet of baking paper on top and roll over that. Slide the rolled-out dough on its sheet of baking paper on to a baking tray and sprinkle with the salt.

Bake in the oven for about 30 minutes; it's ready when the seeds release their oils turning the crispbread brown – just don't let it get too brown.

Allow the bread to cool completely on a wire rack then break into shards.

Gluten-free seedy crispbread

This is a must for your pantry. It's a delicious, moreish snack that can be eaten on its own, topped with cheese and pickles, crumbled over bowl foods like yoghurt with fruits or broken over salads for texture. As it's bound by the psylllium husks and chia seeds rather than by wheat, this crispbread is also gluten free.

I like to make a large batch of the seed mixture and store it in a large sealed jar or container, ready for whipping up some crispbread whenever it's needed.

MAKES 1 CRISPBREAD WITH EXTRA SEED MIX

- 125 G (4½ OZ/1 CUP) CHIA SEEDS
- 125 G (4½ OZ/1 CUP) SUNFLOWER KERNELS
- 180 G (6 OZ/2 CUPS) PEPITAS (PUMPKIN SEEDS)
- 2 TEASPOONS SALT
- 155 G (5½ OZ/1 CUP) SESAME SEEDS
- 115 G (4 OZ/¾ CUP) GOLDEN OR BROWN LINSEEDS (FLAX SEED)
- 80 G (3 OZ/1 CUP) PSYLLIUM HUSKS
- 2 TABLESPOONS RAPESEED OIL

Preheat the oven to 170°C (340°F/Gas 3).

Mix together all the ingredients, except for the rapeseed oil, in a suitable container.

Measure out 195 g(7 oz/2 cups) of the seed mixture and add to a large bowl. Transfer the remaining seed mixture to a sealable container or jar for later use (this quantity will give you enough to make a further 3 crispbreads).

Add 250 ml (9 fl oz/1 cup) of water and the oil to a bowl and stir through the seed mix. Leave to sit for 15 minutes.

Using a spatula, pile the mixture into the centre of a sheet of baking paper, then spread it out into a rectangular shape. Lay a second sheet of baking paper on top and roll over that to roll the mixture out into a 20 cm x 30 cm (8 in x 12 in) rectangle with a thickness of no more than 1 cm (½ in).

Bake in the oven for 45 minutes, or until the edges curl up and start to turn golden brown.

Leave the bread to cool on a wire rack to dry out and become crisp. Store in a sealed container for up to a week.

Danish rye bread

Rye bread to a Dane is like a baguette to a Frenchman. Although, outside of Denmark, and unlike the classic French stick, there seem to be endless techniques and combinations of ingredients in countless recipes for this iconic rye flour loaf. Everyone has a favourite – from pale off-white fluffy versions to those taking up to five days to complete and that end up weighing a ton. There are a few golden rules though: real Danish rye bread must use cracked rye (broken rye kernels), it must be heavy, when sliced, it should have an almost waxy, al dente interior, from the seeds and grains, and the flavour must be a deep malty one.

Rye is a variety of grass similar to wheat and barley. It is grown extensively as a grain crop in Northern Europe and Canada; the reason being it is very hardy and more tolerant to cold temperatures than other grains. It is rich in soluble fibre making it nice and healthy, but being low in gluten means it doesn't rise well – giving the bread its famously dense texture.

On the following pages are two rye bread recipes: the authentic and a slightly simpler version. Both deliver a great bread, perfect for *smørrebrød* (open sandwiches) (see pages 72–5).

The real deal rye bread uses a sourdough starter, which helps the dough bind together and gives it a deeper flavour. Because you have chosen to embark on this mission the reward is two loaves! It also freezes well.

If you keep feeding your starter you can use it every time you want to make rye bread. Stockholm even has a 'starter hotel' where locals leave their starters when they go on holiday to be fed by a baker!

Authentic Danish rye bread

Rye bread sourdough starter

MAKES 800 G (1 LB 12 OZ)

Mix all the starter ingredients together in a bowl with a generous pinch of salt. It should have a wet mud-like consistency. Cover the bowl with plastic wrap and punch some holes in the plastic wrap so the starter can breathe. Leave at room temperature for 2 days.

On the third day, feed the starter by stirring through the rye flour and cold water. Leave for another day or two in the same manner, until it starts bubbling. Now it's ready!

You can store this sourdough starter in the refrigerator. Every week discard half of the starter. Then add 125 ml (4 fl oz/½ cup) water and just 220 g (8 oz) plain (all-purpose) flour. Be sure to mix in some air while combining these and leave at room temperature for a couple of hours before returning to the refrigerator.

250 G (9 OZ/1⅔ CUPS) COARSE WHOLEMEAL RYE FLOUR

400 ML (13½ FL OZ) WARM WATER

2 TABLESPOONS RUNNY HONEY

2 TABLESPOONS NATURAL YOGHURT

TO FEED THE STARTER

100 G (3½ OZ/⅔ CUP) COARSE WHOLEMEAL RYE FLOUR

100 ML (3½ FL OZ) COLD WATER

The bread

MAKES 2 X 800 G (1 LB 12 OZ) LOAVES

Day 1 Combine the cracked rye and all the seeds in a mixing bowl. Add the cold water, cover the bowl with plastic wrap and leave at room temperature for 12–24 hours.

Day 2 Crumble the yeast into a small bowl and pour over the warm water. Stir gently, breaking apart any large lumps. Set aside for a few minutes.

Using a wooden spoon, stir the yeast mixture into the soaked rye and seeds along with the sourdough starter, malt and salt.

Gradually add the flour and keep mixing for 5–8 minutes, until you have a sore arm and a heavy cement-like dough that falls from the spoon if you lift it from the bowl. (If you have a dough mixer, use it for this stage: it will save a lot of energy. Set it on the lowest speed for 8 minutes, scraping down the side regularly.)

Grease the insides of two 25 cm x 10 cm (10 in x 4 in) loaf (bar) tins with sunflower oil. Divide the dough between the tins and smooth over the tops. Keep in a very warm place for 2½ hours to rise.

300 G (10½ OZ) CRACKED RYE

100 G (3½ OZ) PEPTITAS (PUMPKIN SEEDS)

50 G (1¾ OZ) LINSEEDS (FLAX SEEDS)

50 G (1¾ OZ) SUNFLOWER SEEDS

500 ML (17 FL OZ/2 CUPS) COLD WATER

25 G (1 OZ) FRESH YEAST

200 ML (7 FL OZ) WARM WATER

400 G (14 OZ) WET SOURDOUGH STARTER (SEE ABOVE)

2 TABLESPOONS MALT (SEE PAGES 296–7)

20 G (¾ OZ) SALT

400 G (14 OZ/4 CUPS) COARSE WHOLEMEAL RYE FLOUR

SUNFLOWER OIL, FOR GREASING

When you're ready to bake the breads, preheat the oven to 180°C (350°F) and cook the loaves for 1 hour 10 minutes. They won't have risen dramatically but there should be a visible crack along the top of each loaf.

Turn the loaves out of their tins on to a wire rack. If their bases or sides are still a bit moist, cook the breads upside down without their tins in the oven for a further 5 minutes. Allow to cool completely on a wire rack. This can take 2–3 hours depending on the environment.

A simpler Danish rye bread

This is an easy recipe that doesn't require a starter, unlike the authentic version (see pages 231–3). You need to leave the rye and seeds to soak for 24 hours so begin making it the day before you need it.

MAKES 1 X 800 G (1 LB 12 OZ) LOAF

- 150 G (5½ OZ) CRACKED RYE
- 75 G (2¾ OZ) SUNFLOWER SEEDS
- 75 G (2¾ OZ) LINSEEDS (FLAX SEEDS)
- 480 ML (16 FL OZ) COLD WATER
- 250 G (9 OZ/1⅔ CUPS) WHOLEMEAL RYE FLOUR
- ½ TEASPOON DRIED INSTANT YEAST
- 2 TEASPOONS SALT
- 1½ TABLESPOONS GOLDEN SYRUP OR HONEY
- 1 TABLESPOON MALT (SEE PAGES 296–7)
- SUNFLOWER OIL, FOR GREASING

Day 1 Combine the cracked rye, sunflower seeds and linseeds together in a bowl with 300 ml (10 fl oz) of the water. Cover with a clean tea towel (dish towel), lid or plastic wrap, but don't make it airtight, and leave to soak at room temperature for 18–24 hours.

In a second bowl, mix the wholemeal rye flour with the yeast and the remaining 180 ml (6 fl oz) of cold water. Cover with a clean tea towel and set aside at room temperature for 18–24 hours.

Day 2 Combine the two mixtures together, adding the salt, golden syrup or honey, and malt. Knead together thoroughly for at least 5 minutes; all the ingredients need to be well combined and evenly distributed. The dough will be wet, like cement, and it should fall off your hands if held up.

Grease a 25 cm x 10 cm (10 in x 4 in) loaf (bar) tin with sunflower oil. Transfer the dough to the tin and smooth over the surface. Leave in a warm place for 2–3 hours, until the dough has risen to the rim of the tin.

Preheat the oven to 180°C (350°F) and cook the loaf for about 1 hour 20 minutes. It won't have risen dramatically but there should be a visible crack along the top of the loaf.

Remove from the oven and turn the loaf out on to a wire rack. If the base and sides are still a bit moist, cook the bread upside down without its tin in the oven for a further 5 minutes. Allow to cool completely on the wire rack. This can take 2–3 hours, depending on the environment. The loaf will stay fresh for 3 or 4 days if it is stored in a paper bag at room temperature.

Black bread

There's nothing more distinctively Nordic than a loaf of dark bread set on the kitchen table. Each country has its own version made from varying grains, resulting in an array of textures, but they are almost always sweetened with molasses, malt or some form of syrup. This recipe is a tribute to the diversity of grains and flours available on the Nordic supermarket shelf. While it cheats a little with the use of baking soda, you cannot tell from the end product. Persevere in finding the ingredients and you will have a truly delicious loaf.

MAKES 2 X 800 G (1 LB 12 OZ) LOAVES OR 1 X 1.6 KG (3½ LB) LOAF

300 G (10½ OZ/2 CUPS) WHOLEMEAL (WHOLE-WHEAT) FLOUR

270 G (9½ OZ) PLAIN (ALL-PURPOSE) FLOUR

80 G (2¾ OZ) COARSE WHOLEMEAL RYE FLOUR

30 G (1 OZ) WHEAT BRAN

50 G (1¾ OZ) WHEAT GERM

140 G (5 OZ) FINE CRACKED WHEAT

1 TEASPOON MIXED SPICE

1¼ TABLESPOONS BICARBONATE OF SODA (BAKING SODA)

1½ TEASPOONS SALT

140 G (5 OZ) LIGHT MOLASSES

350 ML (12 FL OZ) FULL-CREAM (WHOLE) MILK

500 G (1 LB 2 OZ) NATURAL YOGHURT

50 G (1¾ OZ) RAISINS

50 ML (1¾ FL OZ) SUNFLOWER OIL, FOR GREASING

60 G (2 OZ/½ CUP) SUNFLOWER SEEDS

Preheat the oven to 175°C (345°F).

Combine the flours, wheat bran, wheat germ, cracked wheat, mixed spice, bicarbonate of soda and salt in a large bowl. Add the molasses, milk, yoghurt and raisins and mix well. The dough will be wet, like cement, and it should fall off your hands if held up.

Grease two 25 cm x 10 cm (10 in x 4 in) loaf (bar) tins or one 30 cm x 15 cm (12 in x 6 in) tin. Sprinkle the sunflower seeds over the base of the tins and try to get some to stick to the sides too.

Divide the dough between the tins and cook on the bottom shelf of the oven for 2 hours.

Remove from the oven and allow to rest in their tins for 10 minutes before turning out on to a wire rack to cool. I suggest serving with butter and thin slices of cheese or, as in the photograph, with some peas and fresh cheese mixed with grated horseradish.

AKRITS
äkt
AB

Pear, sage, hazelnut & soda bread

I don't understand why pears are not more often consumed. Perhaps it's because their 'sweet spot' is a little less consistent than their rivals. A beautifully ripe pear is my favourite fruit. When baking with pears, I recommend using them ripe.

SERVES 8

120 G (4½ OZ/1 CUP) CHOPPED HAZELNUTS

50 G (1¾ OZ) UNSALTED BUTTER

5 SAGE STALKS, LEAVES STRIPPED

60 G (2¼ OZ/ ¾ CUP) ROLLED (PORRIDGE) OATS

250 G (9 OZ/1⅔ CUPS) PLAIN (ALL-PURPOSE) FLOUR

200 G (7 OZ/1⅓ CUPS) WHOLEMEAL (WHOLE-WHEAT) FLOUR

¼ TEASPOON BICARBONATE OF SODA (BAKING SODA)

2 TEASPOONS BAKING POWDER

½ TEASPOON GROUND CARDAMOM

¼ TEASPOON FRESHLY GRATED NUTMEG

1 TABLESPOON DARK MALT POWDER

95 G (3¼ OZ/ ½ CUP) DARK BROWN SUGAR, PLUS EXTRA FOR SPRINKLING

¾ TEASPOON SALT

2 EGGS, BEATEN

3 X 150 G (5½ OZ) RIPE PEARS, PEELED AND CORED, 2 GRATED AND 1 SLICED TO DECORATE

250 ML (9 FL OZ/1 CUP) BUTTERMILK OR PLAIN YOGHURT

1½ TEASPOONS NATURAL VANILLA EXTRACT

Preheat the oven to 180°C (350°F). Spread the chopped hazelnuts on a baking tray and bake for 4 minutes, or until lightly golden. Watch carefully as they will burn easily. Set aside to cool.

Lower the oven to 170°C (340°F). Grease a 25 cm x 10 cm (10 in x 4 in) loaf tin with butter.

Melt the butter in a saucepan over a medium heat together with the sage leaves. You don't want to burn the butter here, just heat it until it starts to brown and the sage leaves turn a little crispy. Remove from the heat but keep in a warm place so that the butter remains liquid.

In a large bowl, mix together the cooled toasted hazelnuts with the remaining dry ingredients. Break the eggs into a separate bowl, add the grated pear, buttermilk, warm sage butter and vanilla extract and whisk together well. Gradually add the dry mixture to the wet, stirring together well, to form a heavy, wet dough halfway between a thick cake batter and a bread dough. Add a little more flour if the dough is looking a bit wet or a little extra buttermilk if too dry.

Spoon the dough into the prepared loaf tin and smooth the top of the dough with the back of a spoon. Arrange the pear slices on top and sprinkle over a few teaspoons of dark brown sugar. Bake in the oven for 1 hour.

Serve warm or at room temperature, spread with butter and alongside coffee. This toasts beautifully the next day, like banana bread, and will keep for up to a week in a sealed bag in the refrigerator.

Fig & fennel pull-apart bread

Nordic countries have a closer association with the Mediterranean than many would imagine, with retirees and young families alike spending plenty of time down south topping up their vitamin D levels. I can only imagine that's how this flavour combo was born. Two great bakeries I know of in Stockholm who make the best traditional cinnamon buns do so with these flavours – here they are incorporated into a more savoury dough to be enjoyed with butter and black coffee.

MAKES 1 X 800 G (1 LB 12 OZ) LOAF

125 G (4½ OZ/ ½ CUP) GREEK-STYLE YOGHURT

1 LARGE EGG, AT ROOM TEMPERATURE

3 TABLESPOONS OLIVE OIL

2 TEASPOONS DRIED INSTANT YEAST

225 G (8 OZ/1½ CUPS) PLAIN (ALL-PURPOSE) FLOUR, PLUS EXTRA FOR DUSTING

225 G (8 OZ/1½ CUPS) WHOLEMEAL (WHOLE-WHEAT) FLOUR

1 TABLESPOON RAW SUGAR

½ TEASPOON SALT

FILLING

185 G (6½ OZ/1 CUP) SOFT DRIED FIGS, CHOPPED

30 G (1 OZ) BUTTER, MELTED

100 G (3½ OZ) FENNEL BULB, VERY THINLY SLICED

1 TEASPOON CRUSHED FENNEL SEEDS

1 TEASPOON SEA SALT

2 TABLESPOONS DARK BROWN SUGAR

Mix the yoghurt, egg and olive oil together in a bowl with 170 ml (6 fl oz/ ⅔ cup) of water until well combined. Stir in the instant yeast to dissolve.

Gradually add the flours, sugar and salt and mix everything together to form an elastic dough, then tip onto a clean floured work surface and knead for 2–3 minutes until smooth. Transfer the dough to a lightly greased bowl, cover with a clean tea towel and leave to rise for 30 minutes.

While the dough is rising, prepare the filling by putting all the ingredients in a bowl and gently tossing together.

Once risen, transfer the dough to the work surface and form into a snake-shaped log about 60 cm (24 in) long. Fold the log back on itself to create a 'U' shape with a trough running down the middle of the dough.

Line the trough with the filling ingredients then, holding the end of the dough with two ends, twist the opposite end clockwise three times on itself. Filling will go everywhere, but you can stuff it back in the right places once you have your basic twisted shape. Place the shaped loaf in a greased and floured 25 cm x 12 cm (10 in x 4½ in) loaf tin and set aside to rise for another 15 minutes.

Preheat the oven to 180°C (350°F).

Once risen, transfer the loaf tin to the oven and bake for approximately 40 minutes, or until the loaf is lightly golden and sounds hollow when tapped. Turn out and serve warm, spread with butter and accompanied by a pot of coffee.

Rhubarb & rye bread pudding

Rhubarb thrives in cold climates, making it very popular in all Nordic countries. It keeps well, fresh or when made into compote so you can enjoy it for as long as possible. Just-picked rhubarb is a lovely deep red colour and the stalks should be thin. When you handle it, feel the stems springing back. Pick it early in the year as soon as it pops up through the soil. Rhubarb has a distinctive tart flavour that makes it a versatile ingredient for many sweet and savoury dishes. In this recipe it balances well with the creamy, rich bread pudding.

Use a lighter rye bread, one that is called rye bread but actually contains wheat flour, not a heavy authentic Danish rye bread.

SERVES 4–6

3 LARGE RHUBARB STALKS (APPROX 500 G/1 LB 2 OZ), CHOPPED INTO 3 CM (1¼ IN) CUBES

80 G (2¾ OZ/⅓ CUP) CASTER (SUPERFINE) SUGAR, PLUS 2 TABLESPOONS EXTRA

2 TABLESPOONS UNSALTED BUTTER, PLUS EXTRA FOR GREASING

250 ML (8½ FL OZ/1 CUP) FULL-CREAM (WHOLE) MILK

1 EGG

1 TEASPOON VANILLA EXTRACT

½ TEASPOON GROUND CINNAMON

625 G (1 LB 6 OZ) LIGHT RYE BREAD CUT INTO 5 CM (2 IN) CUBES

40 G (1½ OZ) LIGHT BROWN SUGAR

TO SERVE

150 G (5½ OZ) NATURAL YOGHURT

1 TABLESPOON HONEY

50 ML (1¾ FL OZ) FULL-CREAM (WHOLE) MILK

2 TABLESPOONS WHOLE ROASTED HAZELNUTS

Put the rhubarb in a saucepan and toss with the 2 tablespoons caster sugar. Cook over a low heat with the lid on for 4–6 minutes, until the rhubarb collapses. Remove from the heat and set aside.

Preheat the oven to 180°C (350°F). Butter a small baking dish.

Whisk together the milk, sugar, egg, vanilla, cinnamon and a pinch of salt.

Spread out half the bread cubes in the buttered dish and top with half the rhubarb. Repeat with the remaining bread and rhubarb.

Pour the milk mixture over the layered bread and let it sit for 5 minutes, occasionally pushing down the bread into the liquid.

Dot the top of the pudding with butter and sprinkle over the brown sugar. You don't need much sugar here; it's mainly for looks and to give it a slight crunch.

Bake for 40 minutes, until the corners of the cubed bread on top are darkish brown. Serve the pudding warm.

Whiz the yoghurt, honey, milk and hazelnuts together in a blender and serve with the pudding. It is also very good with ice cream or cream.

Cookies

As a child, I remember there being countless empty round tins stacked up in the pantry, all of which having, at some point, contained Danish butter cookies. All across the region, sitting down with a steaming cup of coffee is a popular pastime and so it is no surprise that there is also a vast array of sweet accompaniments on offer. Generally, you will find that most Nordic cookies are made from the same type of dough, flavoured with warming spices, such as cinnamon, ginger, cocoa and cardamom. They are cut into different shapes, and you will also see them topped or sandwiched with jam.

The Swedish, however, have a particular affection for shortbread and variations on the basic recipes are so numerous that each household can probably claim one as their own. So popular is this crumbly cookie that, in the 1960s, a supermarket chain invited housewives to send in their own twists on the basic dough recipe. The resulting book *Sju sorters kakor (Seven Kinds of Cookies)* containing all those recipes can still be found on most kitchen shelves today.

Hjorthornssalt is a traditional ingredient used in Swedish baking, and in cookie-making in particular. It was originally made from deer antlers but now a more animal-friendly version made from ammonium carbonate is used instead. The carbonate has a very off-putting smell when it is doing its thing in the oven, but it delivers an incredible texture: the biscuits pillow up and develop tiny pockets of air inside, which make them lovely and light. Baking powder produces a similar result.

Cardamom shortbread

MAKES 40

Preheat the oven to 150°C (300°F) and line a baking tray with baking paper. Beat the butter and sugar for 5 minutes, until pale and fluffy. Gradually mix in the oil.

Add the ammonium carbonate to 125 g (4½ oz) flour and combine with the butter mixture. Work in the remaining flour and cardamom.

Divide the dough in half and shape each piece into 2 even logs. Slice 20 discs from each, and then roll each disc into a ball. Place on the lined baking tray and cook for 20 minutes, until they have puffed up and have some visible cracks across the top.

100 G (3½ OZ) UNSALTED BUTTER

270 G (9½ OZ) CASTER (SUPERFINE) SUGAR

100 ML (3½ FL OZ) SUNFLOWER OIL

1 TEASPOON AMMONIUM CARBONATE, OR 2 TEASPOONS BAKING POWDER

240 G (8½ OZ) PLAIN (ALL-PURPOSE) FLOUR

1 TEASPOON GROUND CARDAMOM

Ginger & malt cookies

MAKES 15–25 DEPENDING ON YOUR COOKIE CUTTER

Gently warm the golden syrup or treacle, ginger and bicarbonate of soda in a saucepan over a low heat. Stir gently for 2 minutes, or until you see the bicarbonate of soda foaming. Remove from the heat and set aside.

In a mixing bowl, use your fingertips to mix together the malt, flours, sugar and baking powder.

Slowly add the warm syrup and use a wooden spoon to combine the mixture into a dough. It should be cool enough to handle by now, so shape into a ball. Allow to rest in the bowl at room temperature for 1 hour.

Preheat the oven to 200°C (400°F). Tear off a sheet of baking paper and place the dough on top. Roll out the dough to a thickness of 1–2 cm (½–¾ in) and cut into your desired cookie shapes. Re-roll any trimmings.

Line a baking tray with baking paper and brush it all over with melted butter.

Transfer the cookies to the buttered paper and bake for 15 minutes, until browned at the edges. Be careful that they don't get too brown. Let them cool on the tray.

210 G (7½ OZ) GOLDEN SYRUP OR TREACLE

3 TEASPOONS GROUND GINGER

1 TEASPOON BICARBONATE OF SODA (BAKING SODA)

2 TEASPOONS MALT (SEE PAGES 296–7)

180 G (6½ OZ) GRAHAM FLOUR

180 G (6½ OZ) PLAIN (ALL-PURPOSE) FLOUR

200 G (7 OZ) RAW (DEMERARA) SUGAR

2 TEASPOONS BAKING POWDER

MELTED BUTTER, FOR GREASING

Lemon verbena & poppy seed cookies

MAKES 10–12

- 250 G (9 OZ) UNSALTED BUTTER, SOFTENED
- 130 G (4½ OZ) CASTER (SUPERFINE) SUGAR
- 1 TEASPOON VANILLA EXTRACT
- ¼ TEASPOON SALT
- 300 G (10½ OZ/2 CUPS) PLAIN (ALL-PURPOSE) FLOUR
- 20 G (¾ OZ) POPPY SEEDS, PLUS 1 TABLESPOON TO DECORATE
- 1½ TABLESPOONS FINELY CHOPPED LEMON VERBENA OR LEMON BALM, OR 2 TEASPOONS LEMON ZEST

Using an electric mixer on high speed, beat together the butter, sugar, vanilla and salt for about 3 minutes, until light and fluffy. Reduce the speed to low, then add the flour and poppy seeds and mix until just combined. Add the chopped herbs or zest and stir through.

Tear off a sheet of plastic wrap that is at least 35 cm (14 in) long. Place the dough on top and pat it down. Place another sheet of plastic wrap on top. Using a rolling pin, roll out the dough through the plastic wrap to a thickness of about 2.5 cm (1 in).

Transfer the dough to a baking tray and chill in the refrigerator for at least 20 minutes, until firm. (It can be left in the refrigerator for up to a couple of days.)

Preheat the oven to 180°C (350°F) and line two large baking trays with baking paper.

Unwrap the chilled dough and, using an oval cookie cutter around 7 cm x 5 cm (2¾ in x 2 in), cut out as many ovals as possible, re-rolling any trimmings. Transfer the cookies to the greased baking trays, leaving at least 2 cm (¾ in) between each one. Sprinkle with poppy seeds and gently press them in.

Bake for 15–20 minutes, until the edges are golden. Swap the trays around halfway through cooking so they colour evenly.

Let the cookies cool on their trays on a wire rack for 5 minutes, then transfer to the racks without paper to cool completely.

Carrot & cardamom cake

There is not much to say about this cake other than that it is my favourite. It keeps well and is perfect served with black coffee. This recipe is adapted from the bakery of the iconic Rosendal trädgården (a horticultural garden in front of Rosendal Palace) in Stockholm where they have been baking it for decades. The spices mixed with the carrot and creamy cheese frosting represents what many new Nordic desserts and sweets are all about: sweet and savoury working together.

SERVES 6–8

Preheat the oven to 200°C (400°F). Using an electric whisk on its highest setting, beat the oil and sugar together in a large mixing bowl for about 5 minutes, until white.

Keep beating while you add the carrot and the eggs, one at a time. Next add the flour, spices, bicarbonate of soda, baking powder and salt. Mix for a few minutes, then stir in the walnuts with a spatula.

Grease a 23 cm (9 in) round cake tin and pour in the batter. Bake in the oven for 30–35 minutes, until a skewer inserted into the middle comes out clean. Leave to cool in its tin for 10 minutes then turn out on to a wire rack and leave to cool completely.

While the cake is cooling, make the icing by beating together all the ingredients until smooth.

Ensure the cake is completely cool before spreading over the icing. Serve with a cup of coffee or glass of milk.

225 ML (7½ FL OZ) SUNFLOWER OIL, PLUS EXTRA FOR GREASING

310 G (11 OZ) CASTER (SUPERFINE) SUGAR

170 G (6 OZ) GRATED CARROT

3 EGGS

240 G (8½ OZ) PLAIN (ALL-PURPOSE) FLOUR

½ TEASPOON FRESHLY GRATED NUTMEG

1 TEASPOON GROUND CINNAMON

1 TEASPOON CRUSHED CARDAMOM SEEDS

1 TEASPOON BICARBONATE OF SODA (BAKING SODA)

1 TEASPOON BAKING POWDER

½ TEASPOON SALT

40 G (1½ OZ) CHOPPED WALNUTS

ICING (FROSTING)

200 G (7 OZ) UNSALTED BUTTER

200 G (7 OZ) CREAM CHEESE

180 G (6½ OZ) ICING (CONFECTIONERS') SUGAR

1 TEASPOON VANILLA EXTRACT

JUICE AND ZEST OF 1 LEMON

Chocolate potato cake

Chocolate mud cake is always a winner! In this recipe, using potatoes instead of flour gives the cake a rich, luxurious consistency. It is not traditional but, in the new Nordic style, makes great use of the region's most beloved vegetable. Fans of dark chocolate will particularly enjoy this cake because it's loaded with bitter cocoa – make sure you use top quality cocoa powder though, as there's no disguising an inferior product. The potatoes will help the cake keep moist for at least a day or two after baking.

SERVES 6–8

400 G (14 OZ) POTATOES, SKIN ON

2 VERY LARGE OR 3 SMALL EGGS

70 G (2½ OZ) CASTER (SUPERFINE) SUGAR

1 TEASPOON BAKING POWDER

100 G (3½ OZ) UNSALTED BUTTER, AT ROOM TEMPERATURE, PLUS EXTRA FOR GREASING

4 TABLESPOONS COCOA POWDER

25 G (1 OZ) DRY BREADCRUMBS, FOR BAKING

2 TABLESPOONS ICING (CONFECTIONERS') SUGAR, TO DECORATE

200 ML (7 FL OZ) WHIPPING CREAM, TO SERVE

Boil the potatoes (in their skins) in a large saucepan of water for 10–15 minutes, until soft. Drain, then carefully peel away and discard the skins and mash the flesh until very smooth, or put through a ricer. Chill in the refrigerator until cool.

Preheat the oven to 150°C (300°F). Whisk the eggs, caster sugar, baking powder and butter in a large bowl for about 5 minutes, until pale and fluffy. Add the cocoa powder and whisk for 1 minute.

Add the cooled potatoes and combine only until the white potato colour is absorbed by the brown. If you over-mix, the starch from the potatoes will make the batter gluey and affect the texture of the cake.

Grease an 18–20 cm (7–8 in) round cake tin with butter and sprinkle the breadcrumbs on the base and side. Spoon the batter into the tin. It will be thicker than a normal cake batter, so use a spatula to smooth over the surface.

Bake in the oven for 35 minutes. It will resemble a classic mud cake.

Allow to cool in the tin for 10 minutes, before transferring to a serving plate.

Sprinkle over the icing sugar and serve with whipped cream.

Dream cake with barley & berries

Over fifty years ago a lady living in Jutland, Denmark, invented the original recipe for this cake. Her granddaughter named it drømmekage, *which means 'dream cake', and entered it into a baking competition. The cake won and somehow the news spread like wildfire. It's now one of the most consumed cakes in Denmark. An ambassador of accessible new Nordic dishes, Mia Irene Kristensen, adapted the cake by substituting the coconut in the original version with barley to make it a little more traditionally 'Nordic'. The cake is indulgent: a sponge using cream on the base contrasting with a chewy caramel topping! You can use full-cream (whole) milk instead of the cream.*

SERVES 8–10

300 G (10½ OZ/2 CUPS) PLAIN (ALL-PURPOSE) FLOUR

3 TEASPOONS BAKING POWDER

3 LARGE EGGS

300 G (10½ OZ) CASTER (SUPERFINE) SUGAR

90 G (3 OZ) UNSALTED BUTTER, MELTED

2 TEASPOONS VANILLA EXTRACT

200 ML (7 FL OZ) POURING (SINGLE/ LIGHT) CREAM

175 G (6 OZ) FRESH OR FROZEN RED- OR BLACKCURRANTS, OR BLUEBERRIES

CREAM OR CUSTARD, TO SERVE

TOPPING

180 G (6½ OZ) UNSALTED BUTTER

60 ML (2 FL OZ/¼ CUP) FULL-CREAM (WHOLE) MILK

300 G (10½ OZ) SOFT BROWN SUGAR

175 G (6 OZ) BARLEY FLAKES OR ROLLED (PORRIDGE) OATS

3 TEASPOONS DARK MALT (SEE PAGES 296–7) (OPTIONAL)

Preheat the oven to 190°C (375°F). Sift the flour and baking powder into a bowl.

In a separate large bowl, whisk together the eggs and sugar for about 10 minutes, until pale and fluffy.

Sift the flour and baking powder into the egg mixture and fold to combine. Stir in the melted butter, vanilla and cream. Fold in the currants or berries.

Pour the dough into a 28 cm (11 in) round springform cake tin. (You can use a larger cake tin, but bear in mind to reduce the cooking time.) Bake for 40 minutes, or until the middle of the cake is firm to touch.

About 5 minutes before the cake is ready, make the topping.

Mix together all the ingredients for the topping in a saucepan over a medium heat. Cook, stirring, until it bubbles slightly.

Remove the cake from the oven and increase the temperature to 220°C (430°F).

Pour the caramel over the cake then return it to the oven for 5–7 minutes, until you see it set and start to turn dark brown at the edges. Allow the cake to cool in its tin for a few minutes before running a knife around the edge and releasing the springform. Cool and allow the topping to set before cutting into slices. Serve with cream or custard.

Smoky quinoa & cacao bars

Smoke finds its way into many Nordic foods. In the past it was out of necessity to preserve foods but today its primary function is flavour. Nordic folk have developed a unique palate for all things smoked and pickled. The recipe ahead is a little ode to this.

MAKES ABOUT 16 BARS

- **220 G (8 OZ/1 CUP) PITTED SOFT PRUNES, DICED**
- **2 TABLESPOONS COCONUT OIL**
- **150 G (5½ OZ) ALMOND, HAZELNUT OR PEANUT BUTTER**
- **50 ML (2 FL OZ) RAPESEED OIL**
- **1 TABLESPOON HONEY**
- **PINCH OF CAYENNE PEPPER**
- **180 G (6 OZ/1 CUP) PEPITAS (PUMPKIN SEEDS), LIGHTLY TOASTED**
- **20 G (¾ OZ) CACAO NIBS**
- **25 G (1 OZ/1 CUP) PUFFED QUINOA**
- **90 G (3¼ OZ/ ½ CUP) TOASTED BRAZIL NUTS, COARSELY CHOPPED**
- **100 G (3½ OZ) DARK CHOCOLATE (70% COCOA SOLIDS), BROKEN INTO ROUGH PIECES**
- **1 TABLESPOON SMOKED SALT FLAKES**

Put the prunes in a bowl and mash well with a fork, then add them together with the coconut oil to a large saucepan over a low–medium heat. Stir in the nut butter, oil, honey and cayenne pepper, mashing the prunes further with the back of a wooden spoon to bring everything together. Cook over a low heat, stirring, for 2–3 minutes, until the mixture is soft and gooey, then remove from the heat, stir in the pepitas, cacao nibs, puffed quinoa and chopped brazil nuts and set aside.

Put the chocolate in a heatproof bowl, set it over a saucepan of simmering water and stir gently until the chocolate has melted.

Line a 30 cm x 12 cm (12 in x 4½ in) loaf tin with baking paper. Transfer the mixture to the tin and drizzle over the melted dark chocolate. Sprinkle over the smoked salt, transfer to the refrigerator and leave to chill for at least 1 hour, or until set.

Once set, remove the log from the tin, transfer to a chopping board and cut into bars. They will keep for up to 1 week in a suitable airtight container.

CHAPTER EIGHT

Sweets

'Saturday sweets' is a tradition that has been around for a long time. Every week, children and adults alike head to the supermarket or sweet shop and indulge in all their favourite candy. It began as a government initiative in the 1950s intended to restrict people's consumption of sweets. However, it could be said that it has somewhat backfired, as Sweden and Denmark are believed to be the top consumers of candy per capita in the world.

When it comes to the new Nordic dessert menu, you never quite know what to expect. Given their love of candy, it might be assumed that their desserts would be equally sugary. But just as we have seen throughout the other chapters in this book with sweet elements managing to work their way into savoury dishes, playing with this sweet–savoury contrast is enjoyed in desserts too. New Nordic desserts are not so sweet that they bowl you over; they are often more subtle and you're likely to find some elements more traditionally at home in savoury dishes.

Dairy plays a huge and important role in the Nordic diet, and this is no less true when it comes to dessert. And, since there aren't any tropical fruits hanging from palm trees in Helsinki, the focus is on celebrating the forest fruits. On the following pages you'll find some of the desserts and sweet dishes that I think perfectly combine the use of traditional ingredients with contemporary preparation techniques.

Oats, cranberry & cocoa

Known as 'wheat balls' in Nordic countries, these tasty morsels are very easy to make, keep well and are completely delicious.

The base mix is simple: butter, sugar and oats blended together for as long as your patience can withstand – the longer you beat the mixture, the lighter and fluffier it will be. Then add flavours at your will, such as chocolate chips, chopped nuts, seeds and dried fruit. The resulting consistency should be just wet but not sticking to your palms when you roll them into balls. Depending on what flavourings you add, some may be drier or wetter than others so you may need to add more oats or more butter.

In the past they were usually coated in nibbed sugar or chopped nuts. These are still commonly used today, but the most popular ingredient of the moment is desiccated coconut, which could not be less Nordic! In keeping with the Nordic foraging trend, I have used daisy petals here, which are also great fresh in salads. They have a pleasant texture and floral flavour. These little wheat balls often have coffee added to them and I found that tart, dried cranberries went nicely with this. Blend away!

MAKES 10–12

100 G (3½ OZ) UNSALTED BUTTER

140 G (5 OZ) CASTER (SUPERFINE) SUGAR

60 G (2 OZ) DRIED CRANBERRIES, ROUGHLY CHOPPED

150 G (5½ OZ/1½ CUPS) ROLLED (PORRIDGE) OATS

1 TABLESPOON COCOA POWDER

40 ML (1¼ FL OZ) STRONG COFFEE OR ESPRESSO

AROUND 20 YOUNG DAISY FLOWERS OR ANY OTHER EDIBLE FLOWER PETALS

Using an electric mixer, beat the butter and sugar together in a bowl for about 5 minutes, until light and fluffy.

Mix in the remaining ingredients, apart from the flowers, and beat for around 5 minutes.

Pick the petals from one-quarter of the flowers and scatter them evenly over a plate.

Roll the dough into small balls, each around 5 cm (2 in) in diameter. Roll about one-quarter of the balls in the petals. Repeat with the remaining flowers and dough balls. Enjoy with coffee. They will keep well in a sealed container in the refrigerator. Bring to room temperature before eating.

Strawberry soup, rosemary & feta

This recipe is adapted from a dish I ate while working in Skagen, Denmark. It feels a little indulgent to blend berries in this way but the result is spectacular. Perhaps save this recipe for the height of berry season on a hot summer day.

SERVES 4

4 X 10 CM (4 IN) ROSEMARY SPRIGS

150 G (9 OZ/1 CUP) PLAIN (ALL-PURPOSE) FLOUR

1 TABLESPOON MUSCOVADO SUGAR

75 G (2¾ OZ) UNSALTED BUTTER, AT ROOM TEMPERATURE

100 G (3½ OZ) CREAMY FETA, CRUMBLED

500 G (1 LB 2 OZ) HULLED STRAWBERRIES, COLD FROM THE REFRIGERATOR

Chill four serving bowls in the refrigerator. Preheat the oven to 180°C (350°F).

Place 2 rosemary sprigs on a baking tray and put the tray in the oven; these will be used for the garnish.

Meanwhile, in a bowl, use your fingertips to rub together the flour, sugar, butter and feta to form a sandy crumble mixture. Tip on to a baking tray lined with baking paper and cook in the oven for 5 minutes. Remove from the oven, along with the rosemary sprigs, and leave to cool.

Pick off the leaves from the stems of the baked rosemary sprigs. Blitz in a blender or use a mortar and pestle to create a fine rosemary 'dust'.

Next, blend the strawberries with the leaves from the remaining fresh rosemary sprigs. It should have the consistency of thin cream with lots of air in it.

Divide the soup between the chilled bowls, top with the crumble and garnish with the rosemary 'dust'.

Cardamom rice pudding & cloudberry

I recommend making this on a wintry day when it's windy and wet outside and you are lucky enough to be able to stay indoors. The day I photographed this dish it was particularly cold; it must have been well below zero and my kitchen was filled with the most delicious smells. The nuttiness of the al dente short-grain rice in among the creamiest vanilla cardamom was so good I must have eaten over half the pot.

SERVES 4

120 G (4½ OZ) SHORT-GRAIN RICE

750 ML (25½ FL OZ/3 CUPS) FULL-CREAM (WHOLE) MILK

250 ML (8½ FL OZ/1 CUP) POURING (SINGLE/LIGHT) CREAM

3 TABLESPOONS CASTER (SUPERFINE) SUGAR, PLUS EXTRA TO TASTE

1 TEASPOON CARDAMOM SEEDS, LIGHTLY CRUSHED (OPEN THE PODS TO REMOVE THE SEEDS INSIDE)

1 VANILLA BEAN, SPLIT LENGTHWAYS AND SEEDS SCRAPED

CLOUDBERRY JAM* AND SOUR CREAM, TO SERVE (OPTIONAL)

Place the rice, milk, cream, sugar and cardamom seeds in a deep saucepan. Add the vanilla bean and seeds, stir well and bring slowly to the boil. Simmer very gently for 30–35 minutes, stirring every now and then, until all the liquid has been absorbed and the rice is just cooked.

Spoon the cooked rice pudding into bowls, discarding the vanilla bean, and top with cloudberry jam and sour cream, if desired.

---

* Cloudberry jam is often sold at the large Swedish furniture store (see page 296).

Grilled pear, goat's cheese snow & gingerbread

This recipe walks the tightrope line between sweet and savoury that is so evident in many new Nordic dishes. The charring of the pears actually intensifies their flavour in the ice, and the gingerbread gives some crunch and necessary sweetness to counter the salty 'snow'. If you're not the biggest fan of goat's cheese, I'd probably avoid this dish, but if you do like it, consider it a reinterpretation of the cheese platter.

SERVES 4

200 G (7 OZ) GOAT'S CHEESE, CRUMBLED

2 TEASPOONS ICING (CONFECTIONERS') SUGAR

4 LARGE FIRM, CRISP PEARS (SUCH AS BEURRE BOSC)

GINGERBREAD

210 G (7½ OZ) GOLDEN SYRUP

3 TEASPOONS GROUND GINGER

1 TEASPOON BICARBONATE OF SODA (BAKING SODA)

2 TEASPOONS MALT (SEE PAGES 296–7)

180 G (6½ OZ) GRAHAM FLOUR (SEE PAGE 296)

180 G (6½ OZ) PLAIN (ALL-PURPOSE) FLOUR

200 G (7 OZ) RAW (DEMERARA) SUGAR

2 TEASPOONS BAKING POWDER

50 G (1¾ OZ) UNSALTED BUTTER, MELTED

1½ TABLESPOONS LINSEEDS (FLAX SEEDS)

Using an electric mixer on high speed, beat the goat's cheese and icing sugar in a small bowl until creamy. Gradually beat in 125 ml (4 fl oz/½ cup) water. Transfer to a shallow dish or container, cover, and freeze for at least 6 hours.

Halve 2 of the pears and cook them on a dry cast-iron chargrill pan over medium heat for 15–20 minutes, turning occasionally, until charred and just softened. Allow to cool, then core and blend to a smooth purée. Transfer to a container and freeze for at least 6 hours, until completely solid. (It will keep for up to 1 week, as will the cheese mixture.)

To make the gingerbread, gently warm the syrup, ginger and bicarbonate of soda in a saucepan. Stir gently for 2 minutes, or until you see the bicarbonate of soda foaming. Remove from the heat and set aside.

In a bowl, use your fingertips to mix together the malt, flours, raw sugar and baking powder. Slowly add the warm syrup and use a wooden spoon to combine the mixture into a dough. It should be cool enough to handle by now, so shape into a ball. Allow to rest in the bowl at room temperature for 1 hour.

Preheat the oven to 200°C (400°F). Line a baking tray with baking paper and brush with the melted butter. Roll out the dough on the prepared tray to a thickness of about 1–2 cm (½–¾ in). Sprinkle over the linseeds and bake for 15 minutes, until brown at the edges. Be careful it doesn't get too dark. Cool on the tray, then break into shards about 6 cm x 3 cm (2½ in x 1¼ in).

Let the pear sorbet sit at room temperature for about 30 minutes.

Meanwhile, core the 2 remaining pears and cut into 2 cm (¾ in) thick slices. Cook the pear slices on a dry cast-iron chargrill pan over a medium heat for about 4 minutes on each side, until charred. Divide the slices between four serving bowls. When the sorbet is soft enough to scoop, spoon on to the pear slices and top with gingerbread shards. Using a fork, scrape the frozen goat's cheese mixture until it forms 'snow'. Sprinkle over to your discretion, but go easy, as it is quite salty.

Liquorice, cherries & sea salt

People in Nordic countries love liquorice, but the people of Denmark have a special love affair with a strong, salty variety that has a rather specialised taste. The Danes have a festival dedicated entirely to liquorice and enjoy putting it in almost everything from ice cream to cocktails and beers. This recipe uses original sweet soft liquorice, and I have added some salt flakes to bring out its flavours and replicate the iconic salty version, while the cherries provide a much-needed sweet contrast. For lovers of liquorice, infuse the milk for longer.

SERVES 4

750 ML (25½ FL OZ/3 CUPS) FULL-CREAM (WHOLE) MILK

150 G (5½ OZ) LIQUORICE, THINLY SLICED (A SOFT, NATURAL LIQUORICE MELTS MORE EASILY)

160 G (5½ OZ) CASTER (SUPERFINE) SUGAR

3 GELATINE LEAVES

150 G (5½ OZ) FRESH CHERRIES

1 TABLESPOON SEA SALT FLAKES, OR TO TASTE

Stir the milk, liquorice and half of the sugar in a saucepan set over a medium heat for about 10 minutes, until the liquorice has mostly dissolved. Strain into a large bowl.

Soak the gelatine leaves in cold water for a couple of minutes, then remove and squeeze out the excess water. Whisk the leaves into the warm milk mixture until dissolved.

Place the bowl in the refrigerator for 1 hour then remove and whisk to keep it smooth. Check to see if it is starting to set. If it is still very runny, after whisking, chill it for a further 30 minutes and then check on it again. If it looks like it may be starting to set, pour it into four 200 ml (7 fl oz) serving glasses and chill in the refrigerator for a further 2 hours. (This mixture can be made up to 4 days in advance.)

When you're ready to serve, cut some of the cherries in half, leaving the rest whole. Heat 2 tablespoons water in a non-stick saucepan over a low heat then add the remaining sugar and the cherries and stir together. Simmer gently for no more than a minute, until the sugar has dissolved. Let the cherries cool for a few minutes, then spoon them over the liquorice cream with a little of the syrup. Sprinkle with sea salt flakes to taste.

SVENSKA
JORDGUBBAR
Vikt: 500gr

Almond milk ice, redcurrants & yoghurt loaf

Marzipan is very popular in Nordic countries and features regularly in sweet baked goods. Personally, I don't love the flavour, but I do love almonds. This almond milk ice leans towards the flavour of traditional marzipan without being too strong; the sourness from the yoghurt loaf and the red- or blackcurrants help balance the sweet almond flavour.

SERVES 4

UNSALTED BUTTER OR SUNFLOWER OIL, FOR GREASING

200 G (7 OZ) FRESH RED- OR BLACKCURRANTS

ALMOND MILK ICE

180 G (6½ OZ) CASTER (SUPERFINE) SUGAR

500 ML (17 FL OZ/2 CUPS) UNSWEETENED ALMOND MILK

YOGHURT LOAF

250 G (9 OZ/1 CUP) NATURAL YOGHURT

460 G (1 LB/2 CUPS) CASTER (SUPERFINE) SUGAR

450 G (1 LB/3 CUPS) PLAIN (ALL-PURPOSE) FLOUR

½ TEASPOON GROUND GINGER

125 ML (4 FL OZ/½ CUP) RAPESEED OIL

3 EGGS

1½ TEASPOONS BAKING POWDER

1 TEASPOON NATURAL VANILLA EXTRACT

PINCH OF SALT

2 TABLESPOONS UNSALTED BUTTER, FOR FRYING

For the almond milk ice, heat the sugar and 200 ml (7 fl oz) water in a small saucepan for 5 minutes, stirring regularly, until the sugar has dissolved and you have a sugar syrup. Set aside to cool completely, then combine with the almond milk. Pour into a deep metal baking tray and freeze for at least 4 hours, or overnight.

For the yoghurt loaf, preheat the oven to 180°C (350°F). Line the base of a 20 cm x 10 cm (8 in x 4 in) cake tin with baking paper and grease the sides with butter or oil. Mix together all the ingredients, apart from the butter, in a large bowl until well combined.

Pour the batter into the prepared cake tin, and bake for 30–35 minutes, until the top is golden brown and a skewer inserted into the middle comes out clean. Turn out on to a wire rack and allow to cool.

To serve, remove the almond milk ice from the freezer and allow it to sit at room temperature for 5 minutes.

Meanwhile, cut the loaf into slices and pan-fry them in a little butter until golden brown.

Using a fork scrape the surface of the ice to create 'snow'. Serve the loaf slices topped with 'snow' and the red- or blackcurrants.

Cardamom chocolate cream, blueberries & meringue

In the Classics chapter I touched on the Nordic affinity with cardamom (see page 104). I'm surprised how little this spice is used in other cuisines, particularly in sweet dishes. It goes beautifully with chocolate and all dairy products. In this recipe, the meringue provides a crunchy contrast to the velvety ganache.

SERVES 4

200 G (7 OZ) FRESH BLUEBERRIES

MERINGUE

SPLASH OF WHITE VINEGAR

2 LARGE EGG WHITES, AT ROOM TEMPERATURE

PINCH OF SALT

115 G (4 OZ/½ CUP) CASTER (SUPERFINE) SUGAR

1–2 TABLESPOONS CHUNKY BLUEBERRY JAM

CARDAMOM CHOCOLATE CREAM

100 ML (3½ FL OZ) THICK (DOUBLE/ HEAVY) CREAM, AT ROOM TEMPERATURE

50 ML (1¾ FL OZ) FULL-CREAM (WHOLE) MILK

2 TABLESPOONS RAW (DEMERARA) SUGAR

½ TEASPOON CARDAMOM SEEDS (OPEN THE PODS TO REMOVE THE SEEDS INSIDE)

85 G (3 OZ) MILK CHOCOLATE, BROKEN INTO SQUARES

85 G (3 OZ) DARK CHOCOLATE, BROKEN INTO SQUARES

First make the meringues. Preheat the oven to 100°C (210°F). Lightly douse some paper towel with vinegar and use this to wipe a large mixing bowl and an electric mixer. Line three baking trays with baking paper.

Beat the egg whites in the bowl until they reach soft-peak stage. This is when the whites are aerated and have become white foam; they hold some form but will not stand firm if you lift up the mixture with the whisk. It is important not to over-beat the whites at this stage. Add the salt and continue to beat. Add the sugar, a little at a time, until it's all incorporated. It should now be very firm and at the stiff-peak stage.

Spread the mixture as thinly as possible across the lined baking trays. Spoon the jam on top of the thin mixture and swirl through. There will be a lot of mixture; I had some extra dollops left over for snacks! Cook in the oven for 30 minutes. Leaving the meringues in the oven, turn the oven off and leave the door slightly open. Allow the meringues to cool and crisp up until the centre of the meringue is completely dry and crisp. This can take 1–3 hours, depending on the humidity of the kitchen.

Meanwhile, make the cardamom chocolate cream. In a saucepan, stir the cream, milk, sugar and cardamom over a low heat for 5–10 minutes to allow the cardamom flavour to infuse. Don't let it bubble; you only want it to steep. Remove from the heat and leave to cool completely.

Strain the cooled cream mixture into a clean heatproof bowl. Set it over a saucepan of simmering water (don't let the base of the bowl actually touch the hot water). Stir gently to warm the mixture through then add the pieces of chocolate, and stir until the chocolate has melted and is evenly incorporated. Remove from the heat and chill in the refrigerator for 30 minutes–1 hour, until completely cool and set.

Spoon the chocolate cream into serving bowls, top with fresh blueberries and break over shards of the meringue.

Baked apple, baked chocolate & chestnut

From the very first time I visited the Nordic region, I noticed that white chocolate is a frequent feature on Nordic dessert menus. Like many other ingredients, such as malt, forest herbs and ancient grains, white chocolate has been taken up happily by the new Nordic tradition. One of my favourite ways of eating it is when it has been baked. It develops a strong caramel flavour and crunchy texture that is perfect for garnishing desserts. It is, however, incredibly sweet so in this recipe it is balanced by the earthiness of the chestnut cream.

SERVES 4

2 TABLESPOONS UNSALTED BUTTER, AT ROOM TEMPERATURE

3 GRANNY SMITH APPLES, CORED AND SLICED INTO 1.5 CM (½ IN) THICK DISCS

½ TEASPOON GROUND CINNAMON

2 TABLESPOONS BROWN SUGAR

750 ML (25½ FL OZ/3 CUPS) NON-ALCOHOLIC CIDER

100 ML (3½ FL OZ) WHITE CHOCOLATE, BROKEN INTO 1–2 CM (½–¾ IN) PIECES

200 G (7 OZ) WHIPPING CREAM

2 TABLESPOONS CHESTNUT PURÉE

Preheat the oven to 170°C (340°F). Liberally butter each side of the apple slices. Place on a baking tray lined with baking paper and sprinkle with the cinnamon and sugar. Cook for 30 minutes, until soft, flipping them over halfway through cooking.

While the apples are cooking, reduce the cider in a small saucepan set over high heat until it is one-quarter of its original volume. Remove from the heat and set aside. (As it cools, the sauce will thicken slightly. If it is too thick when it comes to serving, thin it with a little water, using a whisk to incorporate.)

Line a baking tray with baking paper and spread out the pieces of chocolate on it. Cook in the oven with the apples for 5–8 minutes, until the chocolate turns a slightly tan colour. Remove from the oven and leave to cool completely.

Whip the cream to a stiff-peak stage. Carefully fold through the chestnut purée. The purée contains natural oils that can break down the cream if it is mixed in too fast.

By this stage the apples should be ready. Allow them to cool slightly on their tray, then divide between four serving plates. Top with the chestnut cream and crumble over the white chocolate. Finally, drizzle over the cider reduction.

Saffron & coconut pines

Saffron is widely used in Sweden in the lead up to Christmas and with its high price tag it is common to see 'need saffron?' signs taped to the supermarket checkout cashiers, where it is kept under lock and key. Unlike elsewhere, it's not going into paella or risotto Milanese, rather baked goods. This adaptation of a macaroon uses no sugar and is delicious.

MAKES 6 PINES

115 G (4 OZ/ ⅓ CUP) HONEY

2 TEASPOONS NATURAL VANILLA EXTRACT

2 TABLESPOONS COCONUT OIL

½ TEASPOON SAFFRON THREADS

4 EGGWHITES

PINCH OF SALT

180 G (6 OZ/2 CUPS) DESICCATED (SHREDDED) COCONUT

In a small bowl, mix together the honey, vanilla extract, coconut oil and saffron threads to combine. Set aside.

Put the eggwhites in a large whisking bowl with the salt and whisk together until soft peaks form. Gradually fold the desiccated coconut into the eggwhites, then fold through the honey mixture. Chill in the refrigerator for 30 minutes.

Preheat the oven to 180°C (350°F) and line a baking tray with baking paper. Lightly oil a 6-hole muffin tray or six 200 ml (7 fl oz) moulds – I used some cone-shaped moulds but they can be any shape as long as they are around this volume (it's preferable also that they are non-stick for the purposes of tipping upside-down).

Once chilled, divide the coconut and eggwhite mixture evenly between the individual moulds or tray. Spoon in an even layer and press it down firmly with a spoon to compact everything together.

Flip over the moulds or tray and tap if needed so the pines slide out, then arrange the pines on the prepared baking tray and bake in the oven for 15 minutes, or until dark brown at the edges. Leave to cool on the tray before eating. The pines will keep stored in a sealed container for up to 3 days.

White chocolate, blackberry & rosemary mud slice

This slice was inspired by the lovely Sollá, who runs a chain of vegetarian and raw food restaurants in Iceland and who helped me appreciate the potential of vegetarian and raw cooking through her delicious dishes. Indeed, with her five restaurants Sollá has had more success in Reykjavik than the famous golden arches, who were forced to close their doors in 2009.

Sollá's original recipe calls for the use of black beans and cacao, which I have adapted here to reflect new Nordic cuisine's penchant for white chocolate.

MAKES 16 SLICES

75 G (2½ OZ/ ¾ CUP) WALNUT HALVES

40 G (1½ OZ/ ⅓ CUP) CHIA SEEDS

400 G (14 OZ) TINNED BUTTERBEANS (GIANT WHITE BEANS), RINSED AND DRAINED

250 G (9 OZ) GRANULATED SUGAR

80 ML (2½ FL OZ/ ⅓ CUP) COCONUT OIL, MELTED

100 G (3½ OZ/1 CUP) GROUND ALMONDS

1 TEASPOON BAKING POWDER

1 TEASPOON NATURAL VANILLA EXTRACT

¼ TEASPOON SEA SALT FLAKES

150 G (5½ OZ) WHITE CHOCOLATE, BROKEN INTO 1 CM (½ IN PIECES)

2 ROSEMARY SPRIGS, LEAVES STRIPPED

130 G (4½ OZ) FROZEN BLACKBERRIES

Preheat the oven to 180°C (350°F). Lightly grease a 28 cm x 22 cm (11 in x 8½ in) baking tin with butter.

Arrange the walnut halves on a baking tray in an even layer, transfer to the oven and bake for 5 minutes until lightly toasted. Leave to cool, then chop into roughly 1 cm (½ in) pieces. Leave the oven on.

Put the chia seeds in a small blender or spice grinder and whiz together for 20 seconds to form a powder. Tip the ground chia into a bowl, pour over 150 ml (5 fl oz) of water and stir together to form a paste. Set aside.

Place the butterbeans in a food processor and blend together until smooth, then add the chia paste, sugar, coconut oil, ground almonds, baking powder, vanilla extract and sea salt and blitz together to form a smooth batter.

Add the chocolate, half the rosemary, the blackberries and walnuts to the food processor and pulse for 2–3 seconds to combine, then pour the batter into the prepared baking tin. Scatter over the remaining rosemary leaves and bake for 50 minutes, or until it is just set in the middle and the edges are raised and cracked.

Remove from the oven and allow to cool, then cut into squares and serve, or transfer to an airtight container and store in the refrigerator for up to 5 days (they taste even better the next day).

Blueberry & elderflower pie

In the summer months, blueberry and lingonberry bushes carpet the forest floor. Both bushes can be so abundant that a comb-like 'spade' is often used to sweep through them to gather up the fruits into a basket or bucket. This 'spade' is commonplace in most Nordic homes located anywhere near a forest. Small and sweet, forest blueberries differ from the South American farmed blueberries now available all over the world. Their flavour is much more concentrated and sweeter, and this pie is a great way to eat them: gooey, warm and with a little salty, crunchy crust – you can't go wrong. Don't be deterred though, fresh or even frozen berries from anywhere will cook into a marvellous filling. If you do use frozen ones, the pie will need a little longer in the oven.

SERVES 4–6

FRESH CREAM OR ICE CREAM, TO SERVE

PASTRY

180 G (6½ OZ) PLAIN (ALL-PURPOSE) FLOUR, PLUS EXTRA FOR DUSTING

100 G (3½ OZ) UNSALTED BUTTER

2 TABLESPOONS CASTER (SUPERFINE) SUGAR

FILLING

2 EGG YOLKS

45 G (1½ OZ) CASTER (SUPERFINE) SUGAR

2 TABLESPOONS ELDERFLOWER CORDIAL (SEE PAGE 62)

500–900 G (1 LB 2 OZ–2 LB) BLUEBERRIES, THE MORE THE BETTER (IF USING FROZEN, RINSE AND DRAIN THEM FIRST)

CRUMBLE

50 G (1¾ OZ) UNSALTED BUTTER

1 TABLESPOON MUSCOVADO SUGAR

60 G (2 OZ) PLAIN (ALL-PURPOSE) FLOUR

To make the pastry, combine the flour, butter and sugar in a food processor. Mix on a medium speed for about 20 seconds, until the mixture has the consistency of loose soil. With the motor still running, gradually add 1 tablespoon water, until it comes together into a dough. You may need to add a little more flour or water. Alternatively, you can make this dough in a bowl by mixing together the dry ingredients first, then rubbing in the butter and adding the water to bring it all together.

On a lightly floured work surface, roll the dough into a rough disc. Wrap in plastic wrap and chill in the refrigerator for 30 minutes.

Meanwhile, make the filling. Mix together the egg yolks, sugar and elderflower cordial in a bowl.

In a separate bowl combine the crumble ingredients until the mixture has a soil-like consistency. Preheat the oven to 180°C (350°F).

On a lightly floured work surface, roll out the chilled pastry to a thickness of 3 mm (⅛ in). Line the base of a 5 cm (2 in) deep, 20–25 cm (8–10 in) round cake tin or ceramic dish with the pastry.

Spread the egg yolk filling over the base, then top with the blueberries and crumble. Bake for 30 minutes, or until the berries have collapsed and the pastry is golden brown. Serve warm with fresh cream or ice cream.

No bake blackberry & ginger cheesecake

A true cheesecake has to be one of the least healthy cakes out there, so I can understand any reluctance in believing a healthy cheesecake can work. This then is for the non-believers. Surprisingly, the combination of healthy ingredients in this recipe is so rich in flavour that you'll find you can't go wrong. This is no-bake cheesecake uses nuts and dates to make a gluten- and lactose-free version of the classic.

SERVES 8

310 G (11 OZ/2 CUPS) CASHEW NUTS

120 G (4½ OZ/1¼ CUPS) DESICCATED (SHREDDED) COCONUT

290 G (10¼ OZ) HONEY

ZEST AND JUICE OF 2 LEMONS

150 ML (5 FL OZ) COCONUT OIL, MELTED

2 TABLESPOONS NUTRITIONAL YEAST FLAKES

1 TEASPOON NATURAL VANILLA EXTRACT

100 G (3½ OZ) BLACKBERRIES, FRESH OR FROZEN

1 TEASPOON FRESHLY GRATED GINGER

BASE

100 G (3½ OZ/1 CUP) WALNUT HALVES

12 PITTED DATES

2 TEASPOONS CACAO POWDER

1 TEASPOON GROUND CINNAMON

¼ TEASPOON SALT

For the base, put all the ingredients in a food processor and blitz together to a chunky crumb-like consistency. Press the mixture into a 22 cm x 30 cm (8½ in x 12 in) cake tin.

Add the cashew nuts, coconut, honey, lemon zest and lemon juice to the food processor and whiz together for 1 minute, until everything is well combined and the mixture is smooth and creamy. Add the coconut oil, yeast and vanilla extract and whiz again for 30 seconds.

Spoon half the creamy mixture over the base and spread it out evenly.

Add the blackberries and ginger to the remaining mixture and blend together, then spread this over the cheesecake. Smooth down the top of the cheesecake with a spoon and leave to set in the refrigerator for at least 2 hours.

When ready to serve, remove the cheesecake from the tin, transfer to a serving plate and slice into portions. This also makes a great snack to take with you – simply store it in the refrigerator in a sealed bag or wrapped in plastic wrap to prevent it from being tainted by other flavours.

Berry & *skyr* popsicles

While the rest of the world is content with natural and Greek-style yoghurts, the range of fermented and cultured milks in the Nordic region is astounding. But, somehow, Iceland has risen above the others with its slightly sour, velvety skyr, *said to have been introduced to them by the Vikings.* Skyr *is now Iceland's most iconic food product; perhaps not so surprising considering that the world's appetite for whale meat is not particularly strong. It is now gaining quite a global reputation, exported all across Scandinavia and to the UK, and with manufacturers in New York and California in the US. It freezes particularly well, better than most yoghurts and is perfect for these popsicles.*

MAKES ABOUT 8 DEPENDING ON THE SIZE OF YOUR MOULDS

500 G (1 LB 2 OZ) ICELANDIC SKYR OR NATURAL OR GREEK-STYLE YOGHURT

250 G (9 OZ) MIXED BERRIES (FROZEN ARE FINE, BUT RINSE THEM LIGHTLY FIRST)

2 TABLESPOONS RUNNY HONEY

1 TABLESPOON ALMOND BUTTER

Combine all the ingredients well, then spoon into popsicle moulds and freeze for at least 3 hours.

Brown butter ice cream, rhubarb & pepitas

It is said that the Vikings taught the French how to make butter. I'll say no more! Certainly, the interest in all forms of butter and the methods of its preparation are strong across all the Nordic countries. In the Basics chapter I mentioned the current popularity of serving whipped butter in restaurants and cafés. Also popular is the use of brown butter in cooking. Its sweet, nutty characteristics impart a unique flavour on food that is hard to replicate any other way. In this ice cream it provides a sweet umami flavour without the obvious sweetness that a caramel would provide. I don't think I've ever tried an ice cream flavour that I don't like, but this is definitely up there as one of my favourites. You will need a kitchen thermometer for this recipe.

SERVES 4

3–4 RHUBARB STALKS, CHOPPED INTO 2 CM (¾ IN) CUBES

75 G (2¾ OZ) CASTER (SUPERFINE) SUGAR

100 G (3½ OZ) PEPITAS (PUMPKIN SEEDS)

BROWN BUTTER ICE CREAM

100 G (3½ OZ) UNSALTED BUTTER

500 ML (17 FL OZ/2 CUPS) THICK (DOUBLE/HEAVY) CREAM

250 ML (8½ FL OZ/1 CUP) FULL-CREAM (WHOLE) MILK

6 LARGE EGG YOLKS

80 G (2¾ OZ/⅓ CUP) CASTER (SUPERFINE) SUGAR

80 G (2¾ OZ/⅓ CUP) MUSCOVADO SUGAR

1 TEASPOON SEA SALT FLAKES

First make the ice cream. Melt the butter in a saucepan set over a low–medium heat and cook for about 6 minutes, stirring occasionally, until the butter turns a light amber colour. Be careful not to let it burn. Strain through a fine sieve into a small bowl.

Bring the cream and milk to a simmer in a large pan, then remove from the heat.

Whisk the egg yolks, both sugars and the salt in a large bowl until thick and well combined. Add the browned butter and whisk together.

Gradually whisk the hot cream mixture into the brown butter mixture, then return to the pan. Stir the mixture over a low–medium heat for 5 minutes, or until a kitchen thermometer reaches 80°C (175°F). Strain the custard into a clean bowl and set this over a larger bowl of iced water. Stir until the custard is cold.

Process the custard in an ice-cream machine, according to the manufacturer's instructions. Transfer the ice cream to a suitable container and freeze for at least 4 hours.

When ready to serve, toss the rhubarb in 1½ tablespoons of the sugar. Warm through in a saucepan, with the lid on, over a low heat for a few minutes, until the rhubarb collapses. Remove from the heat and set aside.

Meanwhile, line a baking tray with baking paper. In a non-stick pan gently heat the remaining sugar until it begins to caramelise. Quickly stir in the pepitas, then pour on to the prepared baking tray and leave to cool and set.

Spoon the ice cream into bowls, top with a dollop of the stewed rhubarb and break shards of the pepita brittle over the top.

Strawberry balsamic leather

I remember snacking on a processed version of this at primary school. I love how the reduction and drying concentrates the flavour of the berries and I've always loved balsamic with strawberries. It is a great way to use up abundance of fruit that extends its shelf life. You could apply the below recipe to any fruit you find stacking up in your kitchen, just make sure to pass it through a sieve first so you end up with a smooth pulp.

MAKES ONE 30 X 40 CM (12 IN X 16 IN) RECTANGLE

750 G (1 LB 10 OZ) STRAWBERRIES, FRESH OR FROZEN

165 G (5¾ OZ/ ¾ CUP) RAW (DEMERARA) SUGAR

1 TABLESPOON BEST-QUALITY BALSAMIC VINEGAR

Line a large baking sheet with non-stick baking paper.

Put the strawberries and sugar in a food processor or blender and whiz together to form a smooth purée, then strain the mixture through a fine-mesh sieve into a large heavy-based saucepan.

Bring the purée to a boil, then lower to a simmer and cook over a medium–low heat, stirring occasionally, for 45 minutes to 1 hour, or until the mixture has thickened and reduced to about 250 ml (9 fl oz) and stands in ribbons if poured over itself. Preheat the oven to 100°C (200°F).

Gently stir the balsamic vinegar through the hot purée so that it is not entirely incorporated but rather marbles the mix, then pour the purée onto the centre of the prepared baking sheet. Spread it out as evenly as possible into a 30 cm x 40 cm (12 in x 16 in) rectangle using a spatula.

Transfer the purée to the oven and leave to dry for 2–3 hours – the fruit leather will be ready when it no longer sticks to your fingers but is still slightly tacky. Remove the baking tray from the oven and leave to cool and dry completely, this will take at least 3 hours and up to 24.

Once dry, place a sheet of baking paper over the fruit leather, then peel it away from the non-stick paper and roll it up in the new sheet. Keep the rolled fruit leather in a sealed food bag or container for up to 1 month.

THE REPLACEMENTS

A few Nordic products may not be readily available worldwide. The best places to track them down are at specialist food stores or online – or the Ikea food market! And seek out any local community events in your neighbourhood. Failing that, here is a guide to suitable substitutes.

AQUAVIT

Aquavit is similar to vodka in that some forms are odourless and have a mild taste. It is distilled from either grain or potatoes, after which it is often spiced with cumin, fennel or anise. A good substitute is vodka that has been flavoured with these spices, or gin, which is made with juniper – another common Nordic ingredient.

CHANTERELLE MUSHROOMS

These beautiful mushrooms are fairly common in Northern Europe, North America and Asia. Some chefs profess that their flavour is best appreciated in their soaked, dried form, so if you can get hold of some that have been dried, do. In Australia, the closest in flavour is the pine mushroom, which grows in the wild and can be bought at autumn food markets.

CLOUDBERRY

Cloudberries grow in tundra regions, unique to northern latitudes, and in particular the Arctic. Their name comes from the cumulus-like shapes on the outside of the berry. They are incredibly rich in vitamin C and have a tart flavour. The best replacements are blackberries or raspberries, but cloudberry jam can be found at the large Swedish furniture store.

GOOSEBERRY

This berry is native to Northern Europe and has been used throughout the ages. It's not available in the Southern Hemisphere, and its sour taste is best replaced by using fresh young green grapes.

GRAHAM FLOUR

Rather than grinding the entire wheat grain, this flour is produced by grinding the bran, endosperm and germ separately before re-combining them. The best substitute is wholemeal (whole-wheat) flour.

HERRING

Kipper and buckling are other names for herring, so look out for these.

Small mackerel fillets, or sardines make good substitutes; both are a little saltier but will do the trick. Tommy Ruff, which is often called herring in Australia, is not related to the herring from Nordic waters.

JUNIPER

Juniper berries are found in stores that have an extensive range of spices. They go very well in the cooking of game, meat and stews.

LINGONBERRY

Lingonberry is rampant across Swedish forest floors. A small shrub that's low to the ground, it yields tart berries throughout the summer. Its tartness is best balanced by sugar, usually in the form of a jam. This jam accompanies many classic Nordic dishes. The best substitute is cranberry.

LIQUORICE POWDER

This powder ground from the liquorice root can be found in specialty food stores. It can be used to add flavour in cooking sweet and savoury dishes. The flavour is stronger than that of fennel or anise seeds.

LOVAGE

Lovage is a herb adopted by new Nordic cuisine, although it has Asian and Mediterranean roots. The seeds and leaves are used and are best replaced with celery leaves from the heart of the celery.

MALT

Malt is made from sprouted burnt barley. It has a unique flavour that is important when baking an authentic Danish rye bread. Don't confuse it with malted milk powder. You can use malted milk powder as a substitute but its flavour is much milder and bear in mind that the milk powder could affect the end result. Beer-making supply stores, bakery supply stores and health food stores are where you are most likely to find authentic malt.

NORDIC ANCHOVIES

The anchovies used in Nordic cooking differ from those from the Mediterranean. The fish are sprats and they are preserved in a spiced sweet brine rather than oil and salt. Eastern European delis sell a similar product called sprats, which can be found smoked or unsmoked. The latter, in pickling liquid, can be used in place of Nordic anchovies.

PINE NEEDLES

As mentioned in the forest chapter (see page 190) only certain varieties of pine needles can be used in the kitchen. If you have trouble identifying these, you can obtain the flavour from pine needle tea, which can be found in Asian grocers or health food stores.

POLLEN

Dried bee pollen has many health benefits and can therefore be found in many health food stores. In the kitchen, it makes a great sweet, textural addition to dishes.

RAMSONS

Also called wild garlic. Be careful, as it resembles other groundcover leaves that are poisonous. Coming from the chive family it is best described as garlicky with hints of onion. A mixture of garlic, spring onions (scallions) and baby spinach makes for an appropriate substitute.

RAPESEED OIL

Rapeseed oil is also known as canola oil. Warm-pressed canola oil is easily found in grocers but cold-pressed may be a little harder to find. Try good quality delicatessens or oil specialist stores.

RED-, WHITE- AND BLACKCURRANTS

With such a short growing season in most countries, these are not commonplace at local grocers. Sometimes you can find them frozen, but a good replacement would be cranberries, fresh or frozen.

ROSEHIPS

If you're unable to pick them straight from the bush, rosehips can be found in tea bags. Good quality delicatessens also sell rosehip jam or syrup. The next best alternative would be to use quince.

RYE

Rye comes in many different forms in Nordic countries but it is most commonly found elsewhere as rye flour. Cracked rye can be substituted with whole rye grains broken in a blender with any resulting flour sifted out. In place of rye breadcrumbs, a dry biscuit (such as Ryvita) can be crushed into crumbs. Rye meal is produced when the whole grain is ground. Light rye flour refers to where the germ and bran have been removed from the kernel before being ground. A true light rye shouldn't be combined with wheat flour. Fine rye flour (also called bolted rye flour) is milled from partially hulled rye kernels, making it finer in texture and lighter in colour than regular light rye flour. If you can't find fine rye flour, use half regular wholemeal (whole-wheat) rye flour and half wheat flour.

SKYR

Skyr has a slightly sour taste and its texture is close to that of strained yoghurt.

A mixture of strained Greek-style yoghurt and ricotta or mascarpone would be its best replacement.

SORREL

This acidic herb leaf can be found at Asian grocers. The best alternative would be to use lemon balm with a few drops of vinegar or another leaf, such as rocket (arugula) or spinach, dressed with lemon juice.

STINGING NETTLES

If you are unable to come across stinging nettles, or the season is off, the next best option is spinach, kale or cucumber. When cooked, the taste is similar to all three of these.

Index

A

Almond milk ice, redcurrants & yoghurt loaf 274
anchovies, Nordic 297
apple cider granita 113
apples
Baked apple, baked chocolate & chestnut 278
Beetroot, smoky cucumber & seedy crispbread 175
Buckwheat porridge, apple & ginger 54
Duck, charred cucumber & malt 179
Elderflower sherbet ice & buttermilk sponge 210
Hot-smoked salmon, roasted garlic & apple salad 126
Mussels, brown butter, dill & apple 114
Salmon carpaccio & cucumber waldorf 147
Smoked chicken, apple, pickled carrots, hazelnut & raw broccoli (*smørrebrød*) 75
Whole celeriac, whole tarragon chicken & apple 166
aquavit 296

B

Baked apple, baked chocolate & chestnut 278
Baked cauliflower & juniper soup 158
Baked pointed cabbage, beluga lentils & smoked cheese 165
barbecues 28
barley
Dream cake with barley & berries 255
Pork, barley & beetroot salad 169
Bean purée 180
beef
Beef brisket, spiced wine & cauliflower steaks 189
Kalops stew 101
Meatballs 94
Pyttipanna 84
Rare beef, fried shallot, chunky remoulade, dill pickle & grated horseradish (*smørrebrød*) 75
Rare beef, parsnip chips & grated egg 58
smoked 29
see also veal
beetroot
Beetroot, goat's cheese, pea relish & cocoa nibs 153
Beetroot, smoky cucumber & seedy crispbread 175
Pork, barley & beetroot salad 169
Pork, cabbage & cabbage sauce 180
Pyttipanna 84
Veggie chips with horseradish cream & bottarga 157
berries 193
Berry & *skyr* popsicles 291
Cardamom rice pudding & cloudberry 267
Dream cake with barley & berries 255
Ymer, ymerdrys & berries 53
see also blackberries, blueberries, strawberries
biscuits *see* cookies
Black bread 234
blackberries
No bake blackberry & ginger cheesecake 288
White chocolate, blackberry & rosemary mud slice 284
blackcurrants *see* currants
blueberries
Blueberry & elderflower pie 287
Cardamom chocolate cream, blueberries & meringue 277
Dream cake with barley & berries 255
Matcha, quinoa & blueberry sails 216
breads 221
Black bread 234
Fig & fennel pull-apart bread 240
Pear, sage, hazelnut & soda bread 239
Tunnbröd 224
see also crispbreads, rye bread
breakfast
Buckwheat porridge, apple & ginger 54
Nordic granola 107
Open sandwich 71
Smoked eel, leek & scrambled egg 118
Ymer, ymerdrys & berries 53
Brined cod, parsnip & *ymerdrys* 134
brining 23
Brine for fish and seafood 23
broccoli
Fisk frikadeller 97
Smoked chicken, apple, pickled carrots, hazelnut & raw broccoli (*smørrebrød*) 75
Spinach soup, fish roe & egg 117
Brown butter 46
Brown butter ice cream, rhubarb & pepitas 292
Brown sauce 94
brussels sprouts, Fermented 65
buckwheat
Buckwheat porridge, apple & ginger 54
Chanterelles, buckwheat crepes & kale 196
Mackerel, buckwheat & pear salad 137
Malt crumble 179
Nordic granola 107
Smoked pork, peas, pickled kohlrabi, yoghurt mustard crème & toasted buckwheat (*smørrebrød*) 73
burger, Flaked salmon, with parsnip fries & horseradish 121
butter
Brown butter 46
Brown butter ice cream, rhubarb & pepitas 292
Herb butter 134
Mussels, brown butter, dill & apple 114
Radish, butter & honey 57
butter knives, Swedish 16
Buttermilk sponge 210

C

cabbage
Baked pointed cabbage, beluga lentils & smoked cheese 165
Cod, cabbage & smoked rye 144
Pork, cabbage & cabbage sauce 180
cakes
Buttermilk sponge 210
Carrot & cardamom cake 249
Chocolate potato cake 252
Dream cake with barley & berries 255
No bake blackberry & ginger cheesecake 288
Yoghurt loaf 274
cardamom
Cardamom chocolate cream, blueberries & meringue 277
Cardamom rice pudding & cloudberry 267

Cardamom shortbread 245
Carrot & cardamom cake 249
Cinnamon buns 104
Nordic granola 107
Rosehip syrup, baked yoghurt & cardamom crumble 215
carpaccio, Salmon, & cucumber waldorf 147
carrots
Carrot & cardamom cake 249
Kalops stew 101
Meatloaf, cucumber & brown sauce 98
Roast pork, carrot 'chutney' & sunflower cream 183
Smoked chicken, apple, pickled carrots, hazelnut & raw broccoli (*smørrebrød*) 75
Veggie chips with horseradish cream & bottarga 157
cast-iron pans 14
cauliflower
Baked cauliflower & juniper soup 158
Beef brisket, spiced wine & cauliflower steaks 189
caviar *see* fish roe
celeriac
Smoked chicken, mustard yoghurt & poppy seeds 176
Whole celeriac, whole tarragon chicken & apple 166
celery
Chilled pea & dill soup with rye 154
Mackerel, buckwheat & pear salad 137
Salmon carpaccio & cucumber waldorf 147
Smoked cheese, remoulade, celery, pickled red onion & *ymerdrys* (*smørrebrød*) 75
Stout lamb, lentils & cranberry 186
Venison, grilled plums & celery 203
chanterelle mushrooms 296
Chanterelle mushroom mash 199
Chanterelles, buckwheat crepes & kale 196
Venison, pickled chanterelles & mustard rye crumble 206
chard, roe & sunny-side eggs, Rye tart with 129
cheese
Baked pointed cabbage, beluga lentils & smoked cheese 165
Beetroot, goat's cheese, pea relish & cocoa nibs 153
Chanterelles, buckwheat crepes & kale 196
Grilled cos, pear, cottage cheese & sunflower pesto 172
Grilled pear, goat's cheese snow & gingerbread 268
Nettle dumplings, rhubarb & bacon 200
Ramsons paste toastie 195
smoked 29
Smoked cheese, remoulade, celery, pickled red onion & *ymerdrys* (*smørrebrød*) 75
Strawberry soup, rosemary & feta 264
cheese slicer 16
cheesecake, No bake blackberry & ginger 288
chestnut, Baked apple, baked chocolate & 278
cherries, Liquorice & sea salt 271
chicken
smoked 29
Smoked chicken, apple, pickled carrots, hazelnut & raw broccoli (*smørrebrød*) 75
Smoked chicken, mustard yoghurt & poppy seeds 176
Whole celeriac, whole tarragon chicken & apple 166
chicken livers
Pâté, fennel jam & hazelnuts 61
Chilled pea & dill soup with rye 154
chips, Veggie, with horseradish cream & bottarga 157
chocolate and cacao
Baked apple, baked chocolate & chestnut 278
Beetroot, goat's cheese, pea relish & cocoa nibs 153
Cardamom chocolate cream, blueberries & meringue 277
Chocolate potato cake 252
Oats, cranberry & cocoa 263
Smoky quinoa & cacao bars 256
White chocolate, blackberry & rosemary mud slice 284
chutney, Rhubarb 49
Cinnamon buns 104
cloudberries 296
Cardamom rice pudding & cloudberry 267
coconut pines, Saffron & 283
Cod, cabbage & smoked rye 144
Cod en papillote with green tomatoes & dill 133
cookies 244
Cardamom shortbread 245
Ginger & malt cookies 245
Lemon verbena & poppy seed cookies 246
cordial, Elderflower 62
crepes, buckwheat, with Chanterelles & kale 196
crispbreads
Gluten-free seedy crispbread 228
Knäckerbröd 223
Seedy crispbreads 227
cucumbers
Beetroot, smoky cucumber & seedy crispbread 175
Duck, charred cucumber & malt 179
Flaked salmon burger, parsnip fries & horseradish 121
Flounder & Nordic bread salad 141
Hot-smoked salmon, roasted garlic & apple salad 126
Meatballs 94
Meatloaf, cucumber & brown sauce 98
Oysters, apple cider granita & liquorice 113
Salmon carpaccio & cucumber waldorf 147
Watercress crème, smoked salmon, pickled cucumber, dill and chips (*smørrebrød*) 74
curing 37
currants, fresh 297
Almond milk ice, redcurrants & yoghurt loaf 274
Dream cake with barley & berries 255

D

dairy products 20
Danish dishes
Danish rye bread 230–3
Fisk frikadeller 97
Ymer, ymerdrys & berries 53
see also smørrebrød
Denmark 71, 183, 255, 271
desserts 261
Almond milk ice, redcurrants & yoghurt loaf 274
Baked apple, baked chocolate & chestnut 278
Blueberry & elderflower pie 287
Brown butter ice cream, rhubarb & pepitas 292
Cardamom chocolate cream, blueberries & meringue 277

Cardamom rice pudding & cloudberry 267
Elderflower sherbet ice & buttermilk sponge 210
Grilled pear, goat's cheese snow & gingerbread 268
Liquorice, cherries & sea salt 271
Pine, pancakes & pollen 209
Rhubarb & rye bread pudding 243
Rosehip syrup, baked yoghurt & cardamom crumble 215
Strawberry soup, rosemary & feta 264
see also cakes
Dream cake with barley & berries 255
Duck, charred cucumber & malt 179
dumplings, Nettle, with rhubarb & bacon 200

E

eel, Smoked, with leek & scrambled egg 118
egg slicer 16
eggs
Finnish pasties with egg butter 83
Pickled herring with egg salad, radish & tarragon (*smørrebrød*) 73
Pyttipanna 84
Rare beef, parsnip chips & grated egg 58
Rye tart with chard, roe & sunny-side eggs 129
Sill, dill & omelette sandwich 125
Smoked eel, leek & scrambled egg 118
Spinach soup, fish roe & egg 117
elderflower
Blueberry & elderflower pie 287
Elderflower cordial 62
Elderflower sherbet ice & buttermilk sponge 210

F

farming 151
fennel
Fig & fennel pull-apart bread 240
Pâté, fennel jam & hazelnuts 61
Potted trout with pickled fennel on rye 161
Fermented brussels sprouts 65
Fig & fennel pull-apart bread 240
Finland 83, 151
Finnish dishes
Finnish pasties with egg butter 83
Finnish sweet mustard 43
fish 20, 111
Brine for fish and seafood 23
Brined cod, parsnip & *ymerdrys* 134
Cod, cabbage & smoked rye 144
Cod en papillote with green tomatoes & dill 133
Cold-smoked salmon, swordfish, tuna, ocean trout 29
Fisk frikadeller 97
Flounder & Nordic bread salad 141
Hot-smoked fish 29
Mackerel, buckwheat & pear salad 137
pickling 32
Potted trout with pickled fennel on rye 161
Smoked eel, leek & scrambled egg 118
see also herrings, salmon
fish roe
Rye tart with chard, roe & sunny-side eggs 129
Skagenröra, cos & dill 79
Spinach soup, fish roe & egg 117
fishing 111, 161
Fisk frikadeller 97
Flaked salmon burger, parsnip fries & horseradish 121
flatbread *see tunnbröd*
Flounder & Nordic bread salad 141
flour 20
food preservation 22, 41
foraging 13, 193
forest produce 193, 196, 287
fruit 21, 193
fruit leather *see* leather

G

Ginger & malt cookies 245
Gingerbread 268
Gluten-free seedy crispbread 228
gooseberries 296
Graham flour 296
granita, apple cider 113
granola, Nordic 107
gravlax
Gravlax, juniper & mustard seeds 37
Iceberg *smørrebrød* with gravlax & *ymerdrys* 130
Potato waffles & gravlax 80
Grilled cos, pear, cottage cheese & sunflower pesto 172
Grilled pear, goat's cheese snow & gingerbread 268
guillotine, Danish rye bread 16

H

Hasselback potatoes 88
Heavy pickling solution 34
Herb butter 134
herrings, fresh and pickled 296
Herring, potato & lingonberry 93
Jansson's temptation 89
Pickled herring with egg salad, radish & tarragon (*smørrebrød*) 73
Sill, dill & omelette sandwich 125
horseradish
Beetroot, smoky cucumber & seedy crispbread 175
Flaked salmon burger, parsnip fries & horseradish 121
Rare beef, fried shallot, chunky remoulade, dill pickle & grated horseradish (*smørrebrød*) 75
Sill, dill & omelette sandwich 125
Veggie chips with horseradish cream & bottarga 157
hot dogs 151
Hot-smoked salmon, roasted garlic & apple salad 126
hunting 193

I

ice cream and other ices
Almond milk ice 274
apple cider granita 113
Berry & *skyr* popsicles 291
Brown butter ice cream 292
Elderflower sherbet ice 210
goat's cheese snow 268
Iceberg *smørrebrød* with gravlax & *ymerdrys* 130
Iceland 104, 144, 284, 291

J

jams
Fennel jam 61
Plum, vanilla & rosemary jam 50
Jansson's temptation 89
juniper berries 296

K

kale
Chanterelles, buckwheat crepes & kale 196
Duck, charred cucumber & malt 179
Kalops stew 101
kohlrabi
Smoked chicken, mustard yoghurt & poppy seeds 176

Smoked pork, peas, pickled kohlrabi, yoghurt mustard crème & toasted buckwheat (*smørrebrød*) 73

Knäckerbröd 223

L

lamb, Stout, with lentils & cranberry 186
leather, Strawberry balsamic 295
leeks
Chilled pea & dill soup with rye 154
Kalops stew 101
Rye tart with chard, roe & sunny-side eggs 129
Smoked eel, leek & scrambled egg 118
Lemon verbena & poppy seed cookies 246
lentils
Baked pointed cabbage, beluga lentils & smoked cheese 165
Stout lamb, lentils & cranberry 186
lettuce
Grilled cos, pear, cottage cheese & sunflower pesto 172
Iceberg *smørrebrød* with gravlax & *ymerdrys* 130
Sill, dill & omelette sandwich 125
Skagenröra, cos & dill 79
Light pickling solution 34
lingonberries 296
liquorice 296
Cod en papillote with green tomatoes & dill 133
Liquorice, cherries & sea salt 271
Oysters, apple cider granita & liquorice 113
lovage 296

M

Mackerel, buckwheat & pear salad 137
malt 296–7
Danish rye bread 231, 233
Dream cake with barley & berries 255
Duck, charred cucumber & malt 179
Ginger & malt cookies 245
Grilled pear, goat's cheese snow & gingerbread 268
Malt crumble 179
Pear, sage, hazelnut & soda bread 239
malt vinegar 21
mandoline 16
Matcha, quinoa & blueberry sails 216
Meatballs 94
Meatloaf, cucumber & brown sauce 98
meringue, Cardamom chocolate cream, blueberries & 277
mushrooms
Brined cod, parsnip & *ymerdrys* 134
see also chanterelle mushrooms
Mussels, brown butter, dill & apple 114
mustard 21
Finnish sweet mustard 43
Gravlax, juniper & mustard seeds 37
Mustard dill sauce 43
Mustard dressing 130
Mustard rye crumble 206
Mustard yoghurt dressing 176
yoghurt mustard crème 73

N

nettles 297
Nettle dumplings, rhubarb & bacon 200
Nordic anchovies 297
Nordic granola 107
Norway 144

O

oats
Dream cake with barley & berries 255
Malt crumble 179
Matcha, quinoa & blueberry sails 216
Nordic granola 107
Oats, cranberry & cocoa 263
Pear, sage, hazelnut & soda bread 239
omelette sandwich, *Sill*, dill & 125
Onion & cider soup 162
Oysters, apple cider granita & liquorice 113

P

pancakes, Pine & pollen 209
parsnips
Brined cod, parsnip & *ymerdrys* 134
Flaked salmon burger, parsnip fries & horseradish 121
Kalops stew 101
Rare beef, parsnip chips & grated egg 58
Veggie chips with horseradish cream & bottarga 157
pasties, Finnish, with egg butter 83
pastry
Blueberry & elderflower pie 287
Finnish pasties with egg butter 83
Rye tart with chard, roe & sunny-side eggs 129
Pâté, fennel jam & hazelnuts 61
pears
Grilled cos, pear, cottage cheese & sunflower pesto 172
Grilled pear, goat's cheese snow & gingerbread 268
Mackerel, buckwheat & pear salad 137
Pear, sage, hazelnut & soda bread 239
peas
Beetroot, goat's cheese, pea relish & cocoa nibs 153
Chilled pea & dill soup with rye 154
Sill, dill & omelette sandwich 125
Smoked chicken, mustard yoghurt & poppy seeds 176
Smoked pork, peas, pickled kohlrabi, yoghurt mustard crème & toasted buckwheat (*smørrebrød*) 73
pesto, Sunflower 172
Pickled herring with egg salad, radish & tarragon (*smørrebrød*) 73
pickling 32
Heavy pickling solution 34
jars and pots 16
Light pickling solution 34
spices for 32
pie, Blueberry & elderflower 287
pine needles 297
Pine, pancakes & pollen 209
pines, Saffron & coconut 283
plums
Plum, vanilla & rosemary jam 50
Venison, grilled plums & celery 203
pollen 297
poppy seeds
Lemon verbena & poppy seed cookies 246
Smoked chicken, mustard yoghurt & poppy seeds 176
popsicles, Berry & *skyr* 291
pork
Meatballs 94
Pork, barley & beetroot salad 169
Pork, cabbage & cabbage sauce 180
Roast pork, carrot 'chutney' & sunflower cream 183
Smoked pork, peas, pickled kohlrabi, yoghurt mustard crème & toasted buckwheat (*smørrebrød*) 73
porridge
Buckwheat porridge, apple & ginger 54
Scallops, porridge & radish 138
potatoes
Chanterelle mushroom mash 199
Chocolate potato cake 252

Cod, cabbage & smoked rye 144
Hasselback potatoes 88
Herring, potato & lingonberry 93
Jansson's temptation 89
Kalops stew 101
Meatballs 94
Meatloaf, cucumber & brown sauce 98
Potato waffles & gravlax 80
Pyttipanna 84
Veggie chips with horseradish cream & bottarga 157
Venison, pickled chanterelles & mustard rye crumble 206
Potted trout with pickled fennel on rye 161
prawns
Skagenröra, cos & dill 79
smoked 29
preserving *see* food preservation
puddings
Cardamom rice pudding & cloudberry 267
Rhubarb & rye bread pudding 243
Pyttipanna 84

R

radishes
Flounder & Nordic bread salad 141
Hot-smoked salmon, roasted garlic & apple salad 126
Pickled herring with egg salad, radish & tarragon (*smørrebrød*) 73
Potted trout with pickled fennel on rye 161
Radish, butter & honey 57
Scallops, porridge & radish 138
ramsons 297
Ramsons paste toastie 195
rapeseed oil 297
Rare beef, fried shallot, chunky remoulade, dill pickle & grated horseradish (*smørrebrød*) 75
Rare beef, parsnip chips & grated egg 58
raw foods 19
redcurrants *see* currants
Remoulade 97
rhubarb
Brown butter ice cream, rhubarb & pepitas 292
Nettle dumplings, rhubarb & bacon 200
Rhubarb & rye bread pudding 243
Rhubarb chutney 49
rice
Cardamom rice pudding & cloudberry 267
Finnish pasties with egg butter 83
Roast pork, carrot 'chutney' & sunflower cream 183
rolling pin, notched 16
rosehips 297
Rosehip syrup, baked yoghurt & cardamom crumble 215
rye 297
rye bread 230
Authentic Danish rye bread 231
Chilled pea & dill soup with rye 154
Cod, cabbage & smoked rye 144
Flounder & Nordic bread salad 141
guillotine for 16
Potted trout with pickled fennel on rye 161
Rhubarb & rye bread pudding 243
Simpler Danish rye bread 233
sourdough starter for 231
see also smørrebrød, ymerdrys
Rye tart with chard, roe & sunny-side eggs 129

S

Saffron & coconut pines 283
salads
Beetroot, goat's cheese, pea relish & cocoa nibs 153
Beetroot, smoky cucumber & seedy crispbread 175
Flounder & Nordic bread salad 141
Grilled cos, pear, cottage cheese & sunflower pesto 172
Hot-smoked salmon, roasted garlic & apple salad 126
Mackerel, buckwheat & pear salad 137
Pork, barley & beetroot salad 169
Salmon carpaccio & cucumber waldorf 147
Smoked chicken, mustard yoghurt & poppy seeds 176
salmon
Cold-smoked salmon, swordfish, tuna, ocean trout 29
Flaked salmon burger, parsnip fries & horseradish 121
Hot-smoked fish 29
Salmon carpaccio & cucumber waldorf 147
see also gravlax, smoked salmon
sandwiches
Potted trout with pickled fennel on rye 161
Ramsons paste toastie 195
Sill, dill & omelette sandwich 125
see also smørrebrød
sauces
Brown sauce 94
Cabbage sauce 180
Mustard dill sauce 43
Remoulade 97
Smoked cheese sauce 165
Scallops, porridge & radish 138
seafood
Mussels, brown butter, dill & apple 114
Oysters, apple cider granita & liquorice 113
Scallops, porridge & radish 138
see also fish, prawns
seedy crispbread, Gluten-free 228
Seedy crispbreads 227
shortbread, Cardamom 245
Sill, dill & omelette sandwich 125
Skagenröra, cos & dill 79
skyr 297
Berry & *skyr* popsicles 291
slice, White chocolate, blackberry & rosemary mud 284
Smoked cheese, remoulade, celery, pickled red onion & *ymerdrys* (*smørrebrød*) 75
Smoked chicken, apple, pickled carrots, hazelnut & raw broccoli (*smørrebrød*) 75
Smoked chicken, mustard yoghurt & poppy seeds 176
Smoked eel, leek & scrambled egg 118
Smoked pork, peas, pickled kohlrabi, yoghurt mustard crème & toasted buckwheat (*smørrebrød*) 73
smoked salmon
Hot-smoked salmon, roasted garlic & apple salad 126
Watercress crème, smoked salmon, pickled cucumber, dill and chips (*smørrebrød*) 74
smoking 26–9
cheese 29
fish and seafood 29
meat 29
techniques 28–9
vegetables 29
wood for 28

Smoky quinoa & cacao bars 256
smørrebrød 72
Iceberg *smørrebrød* with gravlax & *ymerdrys* 130
Pickled herring with egg salad, radish & tarragon 73
Rare beef, fried shallot, chunky remoulade, dill pickle & grated horseradish 75
Smoked cheese, remoulade, celery, pickled red onion & *ymerdrys* 75
Smoked chicken, apple, pickled carrots, hazelnut & raw broccoli 75
Smoked pork, peas, pickled kohlrabi, yoghurt mustard crème & toasted buckwheat 73
Watercress crème, smoked salmon, pickled cucumber, dill and chips 74
sorrel 297
soups
Baked cauliflower & juniper soup 158
Chilled pea & dill soup with rye 154
Onion & cider soup 162
Spinach soup, fish roe & egg 117
Strawberry soup, rosemary & feta 264
spices for pickling 32
Spinach soup, fish roe & egg 117
Stout lamb, lentils & cranberry 186
strawberries
Strawberry balsamic leather 295
Strawberry soup, rosemary & feta 264
sunflower seeds
Black bread 234
Danish rye bread 231, 233
Gluten-free seedy crispbread 228
Grilled cos, pear, cottage cheese & sunflower pesto 172
Knäckerbröd 223
Nordic granola 107
Roast pork, carrot 'chutney' & sunflower cream 183
Seedy crispbreads 227
Sweden 14, 16, 111, 169, 203, 215, 221, 283
Swedish dishes
Cinnamon buns 104
Jansson's temptation 89
Kalops stew 101
Meatballs 94
Pyttipanna 84
Skagenröra, cos & dill 79
Tunnbröd 224

T

tart, Rye, with chard, roe & sunny-side eggs 129
trout, Potted, with pickled fennel on rye 161
Tunnbröd 224

V

veal
Meatloaf, cucumber & brown sauce 98
vegetables 20–1
pickling 32
smoking 29
Veggie chips with horseradish cream & bottarga 157
see also individual vegetables
venison
smoked 29
Venison, grilled plums & celery 203
Venison, pickled chanterelles & mustard rye crumble 206
Vikings 104, 291, 292
vinegars 21, 32

W

waffles, Potato & gravlax 80
waldorf, Cucumber 147
watercress
Hot-smoked salmon, roasted garlic & apple salad 126
Watercress crème, smoked salmon, pickled cucumber, dill and chips (*smørrebrød*) 74
'wheat balls' 263
White chocolate, blackberry & rosemary mud slice 284
Whole celeriac, whole tarragon chicken & apple 166
whole foods 19
wood for smoking 28

Y

ymerdrys 53
Brined cod, parsnip & *ymerdrys* 134
Iceberg *smørrebrød* with gravlax & *ymerdrys* 130
Smoked cheese, remoulade, celery, pickled red onion & *ymerdrys* (*smørrebrød*) 75
Ymer, ymerdrys & berries 53
yoghurt
Beetroot, smoky cucumber & seedy crispbread 175
Berry & *skyr* popsicles 291
Black bread 234
Fig & fennel pull-apart bread 240
Hot-smoked salmon, roasted garlic & apple salad 126
Iceberg *smørrebrød* with gravlax & *ymerdrys* 130
Pear, sage, hazelnut & soda bread 239
Remoulade 97
Rhubarb & rye bread pudding 243
Rosehip syrup, baked yoghurt & cardamom crumble 215
Salmon carpaccio & cucumber waldorf 147
Smoked chicken, mustard yoghurt & poppy seeds 176
Smoked pork, peas, pickled kohlrabi, yoghurt mustard crème & toasted buckwheat (*smørrebrød*) 73
Ymer, ymerdrys & berries 53
Yoghurt loaf 274

TACK! TAK! TAKK! KIITOS! þakka þér!

Special thanks to my lovely wife, Linda, and our boys, Max and Leon, for understanding the degree of my absence over the course of making this book.

Thanks to family and friends, who I am missing, in Australia.

Thanks to Lucy Heaver and Paul McNally at Hardie Grant and Laura Herring for her impeccable editing.

And thanks to those in Stockholm who helped me with questions and queries: My wife's family, the Andersens, Sanna Liedgren, Petter Viding, Niklas Ekstedt, Göran Svartengren, Sigrid Baranay, Victoria Nordström, Linn Söderström, Henrik Franke, Gunilla at the studio and my agents Pia and Helena.

Also thanks to George and Ellie in London.

A selection of ceramics and tableware used in this book was supplied by these generous companies:

Hay Denmark, Hanna Dalrot Design, Muuto, Gense cutlery, Lindform and Betonggruvan in Stockholm.

Finally, thanks to supreme ceramicists Kasper Würtz and the guy I never met at Skagen Potteri.

Published in 2025 by Hardie Grant Books,
an imprint of Hardie Grant Publishing

First published as *The New Nordic* in 2015

Hardie Grant Books (Melbourne)
Wurundjeri Country
Level 11, 36 Wellington Street
Collingwood, Victoria 3066

Hardie Grant North America
2912 Telegraph Ave
Berkeley, California 94705

hardiegrant.com/books

Hardie Grant acknowledges the Traditional Owners of the Country on which we work, the Wurundjeri People of the Kulin Nation and the Gadigal People of the Eora Nation, and recognises their continuing connection to the land, waters and culture. We pay our respects to their Elders past and present.

A catalogue record for this book is available from the National Library of Australia

Modern Nordic
ISBN 978 1 76145 123 2
ISBN 978 1 76144 352 7 (ebook)

10 9 8 7 6 5 4 3 2 1

Publisher: Simon Davis
Head of Editorial: Jasmin Chua
Editor: Laura Herring
Creative Director: Kristin Thomas
Designer: Murray Batten
Photographer and Stylist: Simon Bajada
Head of Production: Todd Rechner
Production Controller: Jessica Harvie

Colour reproduction by Splitting Image Colour Studio
Printed in China by Leo Paper Products LTD.

MIX
Paper | Supporting responsible forestry
FSC® C020056

The paper this book is printed on is from FSC®-certified forests and other sources. FSC® promotes environmentally responsible, socially beneficial and economically viable management of the world's forests.